HOW TO EDIT TECHNICAL DOCUMENTS
WORKBOOK

Donald W. Bush
and
Charles P. Campbell

D0026482

Oryx Press
1995

T11
.4
.B87
1995

The rare Arabian Oryx is believed to have inspired the myth of the unicorn. This desert antelope became virtually extinct in the early 1960s. At that time several groups of international conservationists arranged to have 9 animals sent to the Phoenix Zoo to be the nucleus of a captive breeding herd. Today the Oryx population is over 1000, and over 500 have been returned to the Middle East.

© 1995 by The Oryx Press
4041 North Central at Indian School Road
Phoenix, Arizona 85012-3397

All rights reserved. No part of this publication may be reproduced or transmitted in any form or by any means, electronic or mechanical, including photocopying, recording, or by any information storage and retrieval system, without permission in writing from The Oryx Press.

Published simultaneously in Canada
Printed and Bound in the United States of America

∞ The paper used in this publication meets the minimum requirements of American National Standard for Information Science—Permanence of Paper for Printed Library Materials, ANSI Z39.48, 1984.

Library of Congress Cataloging-in-Publication Data

Bush, Donald W., 1925–
   How to edit technical documents / Donald W. Bush & Charles P. Campbell.
      p.   cm.
   Includes bibliographical references and index.
   ISBN 0-89774-870-0 —ISBN 0-89774-964-2 (workbook)
   1. Technical editing.   I. Campbell, Charles P.   II. Title.
T11.4.B87   1995
808'.0666—dc20   95-9705
                                                                        CIP

CONTENTS

PREFACE

This workbook is designed as a companion volume to *How to Edit Technical Documents* by Donald W. Bush and Charles P. Campbell (Phoenix: Oryx Press, 1995). The main textbook contains detailed explanations of the principles used in these exercises.

For the most part, the exercises are not "made up," but come from actual technical reports. We have altered names and details that might identify the sources or disclose proprietary information. A few exercises derive from student papers.

Students will benefit not only from doing the exercises in sequence, but from studying (and critiquing) the solutions to the editing problems offered in the back of the book. Professionals can use selected sections of the workbook to hone old skills or develop new ones.

HOW TO USE THE WORKBOOK

Exercises begin with basics, then move through increasingly harder problems. (Here and in the exercises themselves, "Chapter" refers to the main text of *How to Edit Technical Documents*.)

For technical editors, "the basics" means making documents conform to conventions—those of Standard Written English (grammar, usage, punctuation, spelling) and those of particular fields as set forth in field-specific or corporate style guides. Hence, we begin with an exercise designed to familiarize new editors with the most widely used style manual, *The Chicago Manual of Style*. Then comes practice in marking copy.

Still on the basics, we offer several exercises on words, spelling, grammar, and punctuation. Since an editor must understand the structure of rambling sentences, we offer a "bracketing" method for isolating major elements and also some exercises in using transformational grammar.

There are several exercises aimed at developing sensitivity to unneeded words, the excess baggage that makes readers work harder. We also have a series of exercises on different aspects of making sentences work better.

Some of these sentence-improving techniques help in the exercises on paragraph The paragraph exercises include two major techniques for making paragraphs cohe sive (one sentence seeming to connect flawlessly into the next) and coherence (all th sentences together amplifying some central idea).

Finally, there are longer exercises that let the editor act fully as an advocate for th reader. These exercises are compact documents that involve decisions about conte and organization.

There are really no "right answers" to these later exercises. To help you see wheth you got the general idea, however, you can turn to Suggested Solutions at the end. W haven't suggested answers to all the exercises because we want to allow you to com up with some solutions of your own.

We want to thank all the anonymous contributors to these exercises. We hope yo the reader, will enjoy their contributions as much as we did when we found them i manuscripts.

PHILOSOPHY
OF EDITING

How to Edit Technical Documents, the accompanying textbook, is relatively free of rules, levels, checklists, sequences, and procedures. We hope to help you develop editing judgment, so that when you actually edit, you can leave the book behind. The authors even joked about calling the book "Zen and the Art of Technical Editing," since it aims to impart editing wisdom rather than editing rules.

But without rules, how does an editor attack overblown sentences and rambling paragraphs?

GUIDELINES (NOT RULES)

Fortunately, there are indeed some guidelines that experienced editors use to reduce technical prose to intelligibility. For example:

- Eliminate repetition
- Follow parallelism
- Connect with antecedents
- Connect with previous sentences and paragraphs
- Provide beginning frameworks
- Provide emphasis in sentences at the end
- Rescue smothered verbs
- Eliminate stacked modifiers
- Decongest clogged sentences

People will use these guidelines in different ways. In any group, there will be almost as many different ways of editing one sentence as there are group members. And most of the solutions will be right—or at least better than the original.

Students must always be aware that there is no one right way to edit a convoluted sentence. It depends greatly on the context, and on the audience and purpose of the exposition. It depends on the sentence ahead and the sentence behind, which is the purpose of the inchworm linkage (see Chapter 6, p. 61).

THE IDIOM OF THE LANGUAGE

In editing, there are two overriding axioms (again, not rules). Sentences must be logical, and they must be in the idiom of the language. And, as students of English as a Second Language know, idiom is tricky.

Take, for instance, "He operated the machine successfully." Remove "successfully" and you are left with "He operated the machine," which somehow doesn't say much. Idiom seems to demand more. Often the "more" is a time element, like "for three hours" or "yesterday afternoon."

So you remove a word to eliminate redundancy and add several more to satisfy idiom. The difference is that the new words supply information, or insert continuity or emphasis, or provide a bridge that leads smoothly into the next element of text.

Another thing: you must not merely try to make the sentence less clumsy; you must try to figure out what the author is really struggling to say.

Take the sentence:

```
Also shown is an estimate of the percentage of total
personnel effort to be devoted to each of the major
tasks as a function of the quarterly time period.
```

This can be reduced to:

```
Also shown are the estimated personnel needed for
major tasks in each quarter.
```

This revision leaves out "percentage," but it is no less precise, because it points to a figure that is in percentages; to include "percentage" would actually be redundant.

In short, you have to look at the salient message. In cleaning up a muddy passage, sometimes it helps to think of the simplest message possible; that may be what the author meant to say. The world is full of people who think deadwood is elegant.

EDITING THE WHOLE TEXT

As an editor, you realize that editing really takes place not at the sentence level, but at the whole-text level. An editor relies heavily on continuity and devices like the inchworm concept to carry the story along.

In fact, you can't use pronouns or cut redundancy unless you observe what is contained in the previous text. You must even edit troublesome acronyms according to what has come before. Thus, editing sentences is only a start toward learning the overall editing process.

There is one thing for sure: an editor must do more than follow a stylebook and a checklist. You must be a content editor. You must watch for technical accuracy. (See Chapter 2.) You must make the text clear as well as just checking for grammatical accuracy and consistency.

Therefore, to help the author write, you must be a good writer yourself. And if you have to ask what good writing is, perhaps you shouldn't try to be an editor.

PROLIXITY

Some people simply do not realize how bad technical writing can be. For instance, here's an example lifted from a technical report:

> Timely production and delivery of high-quality concise, accurate documentation which meets all customer requirements is vital in assuring that performance of their mission can be achieved by having the necessary reports and documents available when needed and by having all technical information thoroughly documented.

Obviously, some words are not needed. Here's another example:

> This is because there may be numerous satisfactory approaches to solve an engineering problem or to develop a computer system and changes may be desired after the report or specification is already on paper.

These examples illustrate one big reason we need technical editing. Documents must be shaped as well as corrected. This trimming is not just to save space, although that is always a consideration in technical proposals and is becoming more and more important in user manuals. Mostly, trimming is used to help the long-suffering reader.

Too often, editors act like "language police," looking for ways to assert their authority in minor matters of style and consistency. Meanwhile, major crimes like wordiness and disorganization remain undetected.

The better way is for an editor to give in on minor points in order to concentrate on correcting major structural distortions that affect the reader's entire perception. But an editor should not change technical words. This is a common complaint of engineers.

Editors must join the author's team. They must be on the author's side, and work closely with her to make her message come through. Authors seldom know much about "audience."

THE AUTHOR'S STYLE

Something needs to be said about the overwhelming urge to change copy.

Contrary to many corporate stylebooks, the editor's objective is not to obliterate the author's individual flavor and create a distinctive "company style" that will cause customers to swoon. At most, the object is to make company writing conform to the ideal pattern in that technology, so technical customers can understand it and swoon at the ideas it contains.

In technical writing, computer programmers write like other programmers, psychologists like other psychologists, and logistics people like other logistics people, and all of their lingos are quite distinctive. Therefore, the basic objective of an editor is to bring each document up to the high standards used by the best writers in that particular field.

Should different standards apply when thermodynamicists write for managers, or hydrologists for the general public? Probably not. An editor may wish to gloss specialized terms and suggest access tools for nonspecialist readers (upfront summaries, descriptive headings, illustrations), but it may do more harm than good to try to edit out the technical flavor.

On the job, gifted technical authors frequently do emerge, distinguished by their smoothness and sensitivity. Good editors are overjoyed to see them, and seek to preserve that style. They note, too, that good authors stick to the subject and stay within page limits; therefore, there is little reason for editing changes.

But occasionally, too, some author surfaces who tries to emulate Daphne du Maurier or, more often, Lewis Carroll or Mark Twain. (You know, clever humor.) Editors seldom have trouble enlisting the help of the project team in damping that style in favor of hard fact. Cleverness is best left stuck onto the project bulletin board.

In summary, good editors change copy not to outdo authors but to help them, with the object of making documents more approachable, more understandable, and always more accurate.

PART **1**

Exercises

LESSON

1

A large part of an editor's work is making documents conform to three kinds of conventions:

- Style, in the limited sense of matters such as abbreviations, numbers, references, accents, and technical terms. Styling a manuscript may mean following a general style manual, such as *The Chicago Manual of Style* or a field-specific guide. It may also mean creating a style sheet of conventions to use in the typescript at hand.
- Consistency, or making sure that the same terms and abbreviations are used in the same way throughout the typescript.
- Correctness, or making sure that the typescript follows Standard Written English in matters of grammar, usage, spelling, and punctuation.

Following Conventions

1. USING *THE CHICAGO MANUAL OF STYLE,* 14TH ED.

The Chicago Manual of Style is generally regarded as the most useful style guide for editors. If you don't own this important reference source, you should add it to your library. The following exercise will give you a sort of guided tour.

In the space at the left of each descriptive phrase, place the section number (from *Chicago*) where you found the information.

_____ The simplest form of strike-on composition.

_____ The three doctrines of copyright notices.

_____ When it is OK to use two-letter postal abbreviations for U.S. states.

_____ Definition of *recto* page.

_____ Credit lines for illustrations.

_____ Capitalization of topological terms.

_____ Principal use of the en dash.

_____ Permissible changes in the handling of direct quotations.

_____ Recommendations of useful references for editors.

_____ Definition of the term *epublication.*

_____ Punctuating long numerals in scientific copy.

_____ How to query authors on a manuscript.

_____ Accents in classical Greek.

_____ Editing captions for a list of illustrations.

_____ Using a style sheet, with example.

_____ The ideal line length for text meant for continuous reading.

_____ The difference between a *foreword* and a *preface.*

_____ Placement of table numbers.

_____ Proofreaders' marks.

_____ Hyphenating compound words.

_____ History and purpose of the *Manual of Style.*

_____ Alphabetizing, for an index, family names that contain particles.

_____ Breaking equations that are too long to fit on a single line.

_____ Using acronyms in reference lists.

_____ The advantages of endnotes over footnotes.

2. USING STANDARD EDITING MARKS

Use standard editing marks (see pages 114–19, Chapter 11, in the textbook) to make the unedited passage below look like the edited version on the next page.

Unedited Version

An example of bit stream customization given by

Le Gall involved providing random access to, and the

ability to edit, video stored on a computer hard disk.

It was explained that one requirement of such

operations is many access points. There is the

necessity that groups of pictures be coded such that a

fixed number of bits are present to make editing

possible.

The MPEG syntax is achieved by having six layers in

a relationship to each other that supports functions

such as DCT, motion compensation, resynchronization,

and random access point. The bit-stream, which is

characterized by two fields, bit rate and buffer size,

is also defined by the syntax. The minimum buffer size

necessary to decode the bit-stream within the context

of the video buffer verifier is specified by the

buffer size. It is an abstract model of decoding used

to verify that an MPEG bit-stream can be decoded with

reasonable buffering and delay requirements.

Edited Version

Editing video stored on a hard disk requires random access. Also, groups of pictures must be coded so that they contain a fixed number of bits. How these conditions can be met is given in Le Gall's example of bit-stream customization.

The bit stream is customized by the MPEG syntax, which defines the bit rate and the buffer size. The minimum buffer size is specified by the video buffer verifier, an abstract model which verifies that an MPEG bit stream can be decoded without unreasonable buffering and delay requirements. The syntax, interrelating six layers of data, supports functions such as DCT, motion compensation, and resynchronization, and provides the desired random access.

3. ABBREVIATIONS AND MECHANICS

Edit these sentences. Watch out for multiple errors.

1. The desk was five ft., six in. long.

2. The abbreviation for Decibel is Db.

3. Its handy to remember that 1 in equals 2. 54 m.

4. You get less whisky In a 750 Ml. bottle than in a Fifth.

5. The abbreviation of Hertz is Hz; the plural is Hertzes.

6. We can "fix" the trouble in an avg of 5 min.

7. His "farm" was only .06 sq. M.

8. Who is going to checkout the U.S.A.F. pilots?

9. The Vice President - Personnel who was 65 retired.

4. EDITING FOR CONSISTENCY

Check the abbreviations and mechanics in this short sample.

The hood section used was 36" wide and 6 ft. long
at the floor level. The physical space constraints
required that the detector be no more than 12 inches
from the walls of the hood. Measurement points were
chosen every 12 in. along both sides of the hood to
ensure full overlap, and the measurement was extended
one position beyond the active area of the hood at
each end. The detector was placed on the floor for
each shot, shooting parallel to the floor with the
active detector centered 2 1/2 in. above floor level.
The shielding for this detector caused the the
response to drop to 50% at an angle of 26-1/2 degrees
from the center line; thus, the 12-in. spacing ensured
full overlap at the near wall. The hood walls are
formed of 3/16 in. thick stainless steel, with 2-in.-
thick benelex shielding. The attenuation of samples of
Benelex were measured and the results used to correct
the measurement data for all inventory work as well as
for this test.

5. CHECK YOUR SPELLCHECKER

The following sentences have been certified OK by a computer spellchecker. Can you find any errors?

1. By foregoing dividends in this quarter, we can gain the needed capitol for investment.

2. On the advise of council, the comptroller would say nothing about the immanent liability suit.

3. The author asserts that the model of ethical argumentation by analogy is better than Sawyer's legalistic model, but he never revels what Sawyer's model is.

4. Because this article shows how to apply some general ethical principals to dilemmas in technical communication, I defiantly plan to cite it in my paper.

5. The straight forward manner in which the project team presented it's case has lead us to adopt it's approach.

6. With you're circuit board laying flat on the bench, bottom side up, solder a shunt between the pins of R37.

7. Note: the SLAM option effects how the systems conventional memory is handled.

8. Remove the rotor from the mandrill, then inspect the rotor to insure that it is free of burrs.

9. Maintenance of ordinance equipment is preformed in Hanger B.

10. Being unable to breath under the water did not appear to phase the tarantula.

11. The senator's aid, who showed a flare for negotiation, urged the senator to altar her stand and except the compromise.

12. Manufacturing will occur at discreet sights, so that if one plant is racked with labor problems, other plants can continue production.

5. CORRECT GRAMMAR

What's questionable about these sentences?

1. After negotiating the scope of the effort, including cost, experienced personnel will be assigned.

2. Remember, the guest is not only there to be fed, but also to be entertained.

3. When printing, the left margin is shifted to the right by the page-offset feature.

4. It is important that the paint only cover the trim.

5. The list shows what the software regularly sells at, and what the students' purchasing price is.

7. EDITING FOR CORRECTNESS

Correct the spelling, grammar, and mechanics in this paragraph.

The feild of technical communication origionated in reaction to the neglect of tow of Aristotles artstic proofs *pathos* and *ethos*, this neglect caused managers and bureuacrats who needed to understand technical material well enough to make decisions about damn sights and weapons systems to seke *technical writers* who could organize and explain techincal matters. Sometimes these writters were technical poeple themselves; perhaps engineers who did some reading outside there own field and who had a nack (but not a heuristic) for writing pretty well. Others were liberal arts majors who had the intrest and patience to understand and explain technical matters, but who also lacked a heuristic since rhetoric had largely disappeared from college curricula around 1900.

8. ETYMOLOGY

Look up the origins of these words*:

agency	fiscal
campus	fostering
candidate	gamut
civil	implement
compliment	management
council	orient
counsel	professional
currency	recognition
curriculum	recruit
develop	salary
discipline	stationery
disseminate	survey
employ	symposium
etymology	tax
executive, execution	veteran

*There are no solutions to this exercise in the back of the book. Just use a quality dictionary such as Merriam-Webster's *Tenth New Collegiate* or *The American Heritage Dictionary*, 2nd College edition. Better still, if you have access to it, use the *Oxford English Dictionary*.

9. VERBS AND PRONOUNS

Supply the correct form of present-tense verbs and pronouns, as indicated in parentheses at the ends of the sentences. Then justify your interpretation in a sentence or two. (Use "Where Are the Rules When You Need Them?" in the accompanying textbook, Chapter 8, pp. 89–91.)

1. The committee, despite occasional disagreements, usually _____ as an effective policy-making body. (function)

2. Rhythm and blues _____ remained a popular musical format. (have)

3. Dykstra & Malone _____ moved _____ offices to the Vader building. (have, [pronoun])

4. Everyone _____ _____ sandwiches prepared the same way. (prefer, [pronoun])

5. When it comes to salvaging my grade in physics, all _____ lost. (be)

6. One of the students _____ I know _____ playing soccer _____ from Omaha. ([Relative pronoun], be, come)

0. GOTCHAS

ust in case you think technical editing isn't any fun, here are some gotchas that have
ppeared in the literature recently. Can you find them?

1. The projectile stretches the material during
   penetration and snaps back afterwards.

2. This situation is compromised many times, for
   reasons of time, schedule, or cost.

3. Although the history of technical communication,
   like its parent discipline, can stand on its own
   without being seen in an antiquarian sense merely
   as a way to add "color and interest" to "real"
   technical writing, there is no doubt that studies
   of early technical communication would add depth,
   substance, and even credibility to the field at
   large, and to individual academic courses and
   programs as well.

4. Adding more memory lets you free up your computer
   to do other jobs.

5. The greenhouse effect traps solar rays from the
   sun, which warms the earth.

6. The confusion that results from thoughtlessly
   calling a thing by different names seems to grow in
   proportion to the number of words in the term.

11. SOME BRACKETING EXERCISES

FINDING THE MAIN CLAUSE IN THE SENTENCE

Sometimes you run into sentences so complicated that it's hard to discover who's doing what. Here's a way to find a sentence's main clause, so you can figure out the meaning and then rebuild the sentence. **Bracket off all structures that are ineligible to be main structures.** Suppose you come across a sentence like this:

```
It is widely believed that language has an incantatory
power that can, if used in certain ways by adepts, cause
people to sicken and die and force natural phenomena to
obey human commands.
```

Find the ineligible structures by first bracketing off all the prepositional phrases:

```
It is widely believed that language has an incantatory
power that can, if used (in certain ways) (by adepts),
cause people to sicken and die and natural phenomena to
obey orders.
```

Next, bracket off any participial or infinitive phrases (*to* + verb) with their subjects and objects:

```
It is widely believed that language has an incantatory
power that can, if used (in certain ways) (by adepts),
cause [people to sicken and die] and [natural phenomena
to obey orders].
```

Now, bracket off any relative and subordinate clauses:

```
It is widely believed {that language has an incantatory
power} {that can, if used (in certain ways) (by adepts),
cause [people to sicken and die] and [natural phenomena
to obey orders]}.
```

All that's left is "It is widely believed." Since the sentence's real topic is the power of language, you might want to include it in the main grammatical structure:

```
Language is widely believed to have such power that, if
it is chanted by adepts, people will sicken and die and
natural phenomena will obey human commands.
```

Try the bracketing method for the word groups below. Which of them turn out to be grammatically incorrect?

```
1. Although in circumstances that require exception
   reports in addition to the regular periodic
   reports, when the due dates fall within five days
   of one another combining an exception report with a
   periodic report is justified.
```

2. What this particular piece of machinery is is a precursor of the combine.

3. The trouble with that hypothesis is is that it fails to account for all the observed motions.

4. When expenditures made for the purpose of acquiring additional land area for future utilization by the institution are accounted for in the capital budgeting process.

5. Based on an analysis of the effluents being discharged there was a need to implement measures to mitigate the excessive presence of arsenic.

LESSON

2

Using Transformational Grammar

In Chapter 8 of the accompanying textbook, we describe analytic techniques from transformational grammar that can be useful to editors in restructuring prose. The following exercises provide practice in analyzing sentences. Use them to warm up for later exercises.

12. ANALYZE VERB STRINGS

Analyze the verb strings in the following sentences (tense, mode, auxiliary, *have* + -en, *be* + -ing, main verb. See Chapter 8 of the accompanying textbook.) Identify their tenses (e.g., conditional future perfect, past, present progressive), pp. 76–77. If you believe that these sentences can be analyzed in more than one way, justify your interpretation.

1. While he was sampling lakes for acid rain, Carl could have been fishing.

2. Fishing has always been Carl's favorite recreation.

3. By May, Johnson will have become eligible for the health-care plan.

4. Tamara had gotten tired of always being tired at the end of her hospital shift.

5. Marshall is being pigheaded and stubborn about seeing a tutor.

6. We are continually surprised at the condition of the bridges on the interstates.

Underline the verb strings in the following sentences. (See Chapter 8, pp. 75–77, for an explanation of verb types.) Indicate whether verbs are transitive (VT), intransitive (VI), intransitive plus adverbial modifier (VIa), linking verb plus adjective phrase (VLj), linking verb plus noun phrase (VLn), two-place verb with object and complement (Vc) or with direct and indirect objects (Vg), or a form of *to be* plus adjective phrase (BEj), noun phrase (BEn), or adverb of place (BEa).

7. With this utility, making macros is easy.

8. By recording your keystrokes, this utility can build you a macro.

9. The next figure shows a macro that converts user keystrokes into macro actions.

10. Novices may find macros difficult to use.

11. Sometimes a problem appears after many repetitions of the same command in a loop macro.

12. Debugging is the process of isolating and fixing problems in a macro.

13. The macro's problem may be in a faulty keystroke sequence.

14. With longer macros, debugging becomes more difficult.

15. In very long macros, debugging may seem an endless process.

16. At the end of debug mode, the debug window closes.

3. DIAGRAM VERB STRINGS

)iagram only the verb strings in the following sentences.Treat verbs with particles .s single words. On the line above the verb, point out modals and auxiliaries, and ndicate the type of verb [VT, VI, etc.). Then, on a line above that, indicate the status onferred on the main verb (MV) by tense and by modals and auxiliaries, if any (e.g., ast or present, conditional, perfect, progressive). See Chapter 8, pp. 77–81, in the ccompanying text.

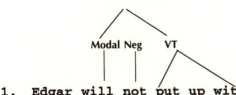

1. Edgar <u>will not put up with</u> his roommate's slovenly habits.

2. Sally looked up the information on morphemes in the *Encyclopedia of Linguistics*.

3. The Garcías had called up and left a message on our answering machine.

4. Marie could have been called in for jury duty any
   time last week.

5. Why were our plane reservations all fouled up?

4. TRANSFORM SENTENCES

ransform the following sentences as indicated. Sentence transformations are described
Chapter 8 of the accompanying text.

1. Universality of access is an important health-care
    reform issue. (Negative sentence)

2. Universality of access is an important health-care
    reform issue. (Yes/no question)

3. Universality of access is an important health-care
    reform issue. (Adverbial Wh-question)

4. Universality of access is an important health-care
    reform issue. (Pronoun Wh- question)

5. Congress is discussing the issue of universal
    access to health care. (Passive)

6. You will write your representative. You will
    express your ideas about health-care reform.
    (Imperative)

7. You will write your congressional representative.
    You will express your ideas about health-care
    reform. (Compound verb)

8. Many weighty and complex issues are up for
    consideration by Congress. (Existential there)

15. IDENTIFY CORE SENTENCES

Transform the following examples back into their core sentences. For an account of some transformations and core sentences, see pp. 78–81, Chapter 8, in the accompanying text.

1. There are no atheists in foxholes.

2. Take two aspirin and call me in the morning.

3. What is the question on everyone's mind?

4. Is Congress capable of passing a meaningful
    campaign-reform bill?

5. How are impoverished students supposed to cope with
    higher tuition bills?

6. Our plane reservations were fouled up by an
    inexperienced travel agent.

16. DIAGRAM SENTENCES TO DISCOVER STRUCTURE

Diagram the following sentences, using the S = NP + VP method shown on pages 75–81, Chapter 8, of the accompanying text.

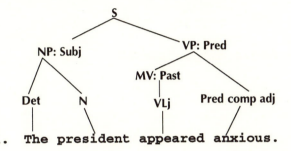

1. The president appeared anxious.

2. The president appeared at the dais.

3. The check is in the mail.

4. Sheldon looks up to his father.

5. The usher found her a seat.

6. The usher found her a noisy brat.

7. The students sat in at the president's office.

8. The students sat in the president's office.

9. Cecilia found George a good cook.

10. Has anyone been reading the novels of Philip K.
    Dick?

11. Today's thundershower could not have been
    predicted.

12. When will you be visiting Provence and Catalonia?

13. Get up and look out the window.

14. There are many pueblos in New Mexico.

LESSON

3

You can improve a document most by working with sentences. Remember, though, that what you do inside the sentence must make sense with regard to larger units.

The exercises in this section draw upon techniques explained in the accompanying text: Chapter 2, "Content Editing," Chapter 3, "Cutting Copy," and Chapter 6, "Sentences with Style."

Improving Sentences

SIX TIPS TO HELP YOU IN YOUR EDITING

(1) Fix sentences to put the most powerful words at the end. Instead of this—

Reflecting the shift from pure commercial lending to a balanced corporate finance strategy is a fundamental change in XYZ's revenue mix.

Try this:

The change in the XYZ revenue mix reflects the shift from pure commercial lending to balanced corporate finance.

(2) Put the verb next to the subject. Instead of this—

Negotiations that could settle the long-standing dispute over water storage are continuing.

Try this:

Negotiations are continuing that could settle the long-standing dispute over water storage.

(3) Eliminate stacked modifiers. Instead of this—

The Schluss Funds offer high return-on-equity potential.

Try this:

The Schluss Funds offer potential for a high return on equity.

(4) Reverse left-branching sentences. Instead of this—

Higher selling prices, record production volumes, and lower manufacturing costs enabled us to achieve improved margins throughout the year.

Try this:

We improved our margins this year by attaining higher selling prices, record production volumes, and lower manufacturing costs.

SIX TIPS TO HELP YOU IN YOUR EDITING *(continued)*

(5) Concentrate on plain old parallelism. Instead of this—

```
Schluss Funds offers you
• A leader in select capital market origination
• Growing strength in private placements
• Pioneered instruments backed by receivables
• Premier agent for credit facilities
```

Try this:

```
Schluss Funds offers you
• Leadership in select capital market origination
• Growing strength in private placements
• Imagination in pioneering instruments backed by receiv-
  ables
• Success as the premier agent for credit facilities
```

(6) Avoid overusing the passive voice. Instead of this—

```
By the end of the year, suggestions from hundreds of
employees that will save customers nearly $2 million
annually had been approved and are being implemented.
```

Try this:

```
By the end of the year we had begun using suggestions
from hundreds of employees, suggestions which will save
customers nearly $2 million annually.
```

17. THE THEME-RHEME CONCEPT

Editors know that sentences are more powerful if they orient the reader with the theme, or the ongoing topic, at the start and put the new information in the stress position at the end. Writers, on the other hand, often begin with the rheme because they're focused on new information. Try these sentences, most of which are written backwards.

1. Cutting the rates at which we use energy is the solution to slowing the process of global warming.

    The solution to slowing global warming (theme) is to cut the rates at which we use energy (rheme).

2. Variety is the key to the plan.

3. Writers should ask if the new learning is job-related or pleasure-related in order to lay out a manual.

4. We also question $700 of the proposed travel cost to attend professional meetings as a direct charge.

5. Seismic activity is one of the biggest concerns in any type of civil engineering in California.

6. The Mobile Servicing Center will be the same size but about three times as strong as the Canadarm.

7. Educating co-workers that AIDS could not be casually transmitted, people with the virus were encouraged to remain working as long as the disease allowed.

8. Spores are generally flattened as the sediments are compacted.

9. Visual problems occur also at the intoxicating dosages.

10. Before the Devonian, lower groups of plants, especially the algae, provide most of our knowledge of plants.

11. Refer to the user manual for more information on how to set the ribbon life.

12. To search for completeness and fairness in analyzing how the process of schooling is linked to cultivation of reasoning is the objective of school reform.

13. The right not to be treated as if one were a mere resource or instrument is most fundamentally what it means to say that one has rights.

14. Today, with the new technologies, no one can afford
    to take a simplistic view of the problem.
    Everything from physical security and backup media
    to learning curves and cutover routines must be
    considered. In some cases, numerous technical
    problems as well as cultural barriers must be
    overcome.

18. FRAMEWORK

As part of the theme-rheme concept, place the framework before the action. This is particularly pertinent in writing manuals. "When the red lamp lights, start the printing sequence." Here are some practice sentences.

1. Check your position immediately after you make your response.

   After you respond, check your position immediately.

2. You should see a small glass tube, which is the level indicator, after you remove the inspection cover.

3. Users will want to change their passwords as soon as they log onto the system for the first time.

4. Grip two of the tripod legs, one in each hand, after having set the third leg in the ground about 18 in. from the transit station.

5. Resume pressure if bleeding occurs and hold for 5 minutes.

6. Contact George Jones at 555-4630 (evenings and weekends) if you have any questions or want more information about interacting with other technical communicators.

7. Do not touch components or flex the board during removal/installation.

8. Verify that all the procedures in the previous chapter have been completed before loading the paper.

9. Portions of the final library site will be fenced off to allow work to proceed in a safe manner.

10. The nitrogen dioxide undergoes a transformation once in contact with an ozone molecule, robbing the weaker, more unstable ozone molecule of an oxygen atom, destroying the ozone molecule, which then becomes a normal oxygen atom, O_2.

19. SMOTHERED VERBS

One of an editor's neatest tricks is releasing "smothered" verbs, allowing them to breathe again. Smothered verbs (sometimes called *nominalizations*) are verbs that have been transformed into nouns, often acquiring the ending "tion" or "ment." Releasing them makes copy shorter and more active. Here are some exercises to try.

1. When application of pressure is employed by the operator, release of the pin is accomplished.

   When the operator applies pressure, the pin releases.

2. All plane landings and ship dockings will have to be done in a controlled manner.

3. Summarization will be in a form capable of being self-interpretive, and at the same time, capable of being compared with other phases of the program.

4. The implementation of the rule necessitated reconsideration of the policies.

5. Many functions of the PC and the Macintosh are similar, so our expectation is that conversion will result in a minimization of confusion.

6. This process has the potential of a 30% cost decrease over machined parts.

7. A summary of the major impacts on plant operation
   is given below.

8. When the drying of the hair is complete, you can
   apply the spray glue with the assistance of a curry
   comb.

9. Even though a significant improvement is attained
   in application operations, certain inherent
   weaknesses in the system may at some time
   accumulate to the point where the use requirements
   will be compromised and the reliability of the
   system degraded.

10. One area of concern evident in this development is
    recognition by community and professional leaders
    that the rapid expansion of knowledge in the.
    communications and resource infrastructure field
    will require full time study and necessitate
    resolution of issues of staffing and finance.

11. See Section 4 for a description of the calibration
    process employed on the system.

12. During installation, connection must be made from
    the serial port B to the rear left intermediate
    cage connector.

20. MOVE THE VERB

Improve these sentences by either moving the verb or correcting its "smothered" status.

1. A packaging concept based on the use of surface-mounted electronic components and a high-density multilayer substrate is in development by Division G-7.

2. Air plans describing a typical flying day of cyclic operations were developed for the aviation ships.

3. The value of a light carrier with a multimission air wing aboard as a supplement to the carrier task force is demonstrated.

4. A description of the types of presentation methods is given.

5. Removal and installation of components, testing, adjustment, inspection, and servicing are also included in the course.

6. A detailed review of the cost elements of the
    contract will be conducted.

7. As each up aircraft flew and returned, an "up" or
    "down" status, based on the mean times between
    maintenance actions, was computed.

21. VERBS AND EDITING

Rewrite in the simplest manner possible.

1. Voice communication needs may indicate the incorporation of a telephone or intercom.

2. Magnification, image rotation, and illumination are the most significant factors in the design of optical viewing systems.

3. Our objective is to be timely in meeting schedules for information and data supplied to others.

4. We plan to initiate and implement a personnel training program to assure our personnel achieve or maintain the minimum skills.

5. Data conversion from graphics models to the format required is accomplished by the computer by use of preprogrammed rules.

6. Real-time transmission of inflight events and
    displays is possible.

7. Lack of flatness on the large planar surfaces,
    uneven thicknesses, and edge rounding are the
    principal conditions that can preclude the use of
    chem milling as a finishing operation.

22. SEPARATE VERBS FOR CLARITY

Separate the actions in the following sentences.

1. Plug in and turn on the power strip for the work station.

   Plug in the work station and turn on the power strip.

2. F-6 and F-8 have resumed their high-angle-of-attack and roll-rate programs, respectively.

3. The chapter newsletter is one of the primary means of communicating news and events about and developing interest in the society at the local and international levels.

4. We need to judge the quality of proposals prepared by or with input from technical communicators.

5. You should first know the location and understand the earthquake potential of the major faults.

6. The requirement for and magnitude of the orbital propulsion system will vary according to the type of flight trajectory vehicle configuration and accuracy requirements.

23. STACKED MODIFIERS

Technical authors have a tendency to stack noun modifiers ahead of their nouns. The remedy is to loosen up the sentences with a few prepositional phrases, starting at the right end of the noun stack. Here are a few sentences for you to try.

1. FORTRAN uses segmented functional unit vector processors.

    FORTRAN processes vectors in units segmented by function.

2. In 1953, Coalinga suffered from a high VIII to low IX intensity earthquake.

3. One cannot help but wonder about the software manufacturer's hardware system configuration philosophy.

4. Titanium will also be competitive on a life cycle cost basis if reduced corrosion control maintenance is considered.

5. Partial-wave left-right asymmetry measurement was accomplished by means of a polarized proton target experimental setup.

6. Gaza Technics, Inc., is building a silicon chip selenium coating assembly line.

7. A protocol is a computer to computer information transfer network language.

24. RIGHT-BRANCHING

Improve these sentences by shifting the lists toward the end.

1. The physically active child will have his share of spills, bumps, and bruises during this period.

2. With the XYZ recorder, pay-per-view movies, concerts, sporting events, etc., will be available for you to watch.

3. The conditions in general—lack of exercise, isolation from other animals, lengthy confinement in tiny cages—are stressful.

4. One doctrine states that punishment deters as its certainty, severity, and promptness increase.

5. By offering education concerning transmission of AIDS, through public service announcements, industry bulletins, and workplace discussion groups, some of the panic concerning AIDS may be diminished.

6. Three watertight openings house the mode, set, and light function buttons located on the side of the watch body.

7. More narrowly targeted gun control measures, like gunowner licensing and permit-to-purchase systems, seem more advisable than having a complete gun control law passed.

8. The emergence of a "codependent" self is common among adults who grew up in troubled families, where chronic physical or mental illness, sexual, verbal, emotional, and physical abuse, alcoholism, rigidity, coldness, or lack of nurturing were common.

9. In the chrono mode, the screen displays stopwatch time, beginning at 00.00.00, showing hours, minutes, and seconds.

10. Many significant surface features, such as apertures (openings through the walls) and the number, shape, length or size, arrangement, and modifications, are among the most diagnostic features.

25. PARALLELISM

The single most frequent structural problem an editor faces may be lack of parallelism.
Create parallelism in the following sentences.

1. The paper is well organized, clear, and represents
   an important area in current policy.

2. The concern of many technical writers is how to
   keep up with changing technology--both in the tools
   they use as well as the subject matter.

3. Start up, run, and shut down the 3456 tester.
   a. Load and unload in-circuit test programs.
   b. Operational verification program.
   c. Identify fixture for items under test.
   d. Electrostatic device protection.

4. Additional budget is required in order to cover (1)
   unexpected liaison to obtain the test specimen and
   (2) dummy electronic boxes from a CNI-shelf test
   were to be used for this test but differences in
   the mounting techniques required a redesign of one
   dummy box and extensive rework of the other.

5. Beginners in private accounting can start as ledger
   or cost clerks, timekeepers, or junior internal
   auditors, in addition to train for technical and
   executive positions.

6. Arc voltage control for maintaining constant arc
   lengths, magnetic arc oscillation and
   stabilization, and a seam tracker for automatically
   positioning the torch over the joint are all used
   when necessary.

26. CREATE MORE PUNCH IN THESE SENTENCES

Try putting the framework at the start, eliminating smothered verbs, using the theme-rheme concept, using right-branching, and cutting words.

1. He discusses the deaths related to drunk driving in his book, *Drinking Driving*.

2. Copper-clad, glass-epoxy board is by far the most popular substrate material in use today.

3. The mere mention of AIDS causes panic in many people.

4. Both marine and terragenous fossils are generally mixed in beach and shelf deposits.

5. In many cases, the homeless adopt bizarre behavior patterns out of fear and depression.

6. NASA could scrap the program entirely, if its Space Station budget is too low.

7. In New York City, 75% of drivers who are fatally injured have been drinking and 46% have an alcohol concentration of 0.25 or higher in their blood.

8. Water or cleaning chemicals retained in the pores of the dielectric will cause the insulation resistance of the material to decrease.

9. The Orlando police department trained more than 2,500 women to use guns in two years.

10. In a 1976 survey in India the preference between the different types of English were questioned from a number of faculty and students at several colleges and universities.

11. Another symptom among the homeless is paranoia, the feeling that people are out to harm them. In reality, the opposite is true. No one is even available to help.

12. Laboratory sampling, inspecting, and preparing of plant microfossils is done in separate steps and locations.

13. According to the U.S. Bureau of Justice, only 20
    people were legally executed, all for murders,
    between the years 1967-1984.

14. Structural extensions, two more crew members, and a
    service track assembly are other possible additions
    to the shuttle.

27. MARATHON SENTENCES

Analyze these long sentences to determine how they could be dissected for more efficient reading.

1. Undeniable though it may be that words are powerful symbols of feeling and attitude and, as such, solid parts of the social structure and that, for this reason, reformers are from time to time tempted to try to amend and change the language to remedy social inequalities, it is nevertheless also necessary to recognize that because language has the force of history behind it, any such attempts to change society by censoring the language are unlikely to meet with a great deal of success.

2. Used as an adjunct or research method in a field such as technical writing, history can play a secondary role in two main ways: first by providing examples of early works in the field, thereby broadening our knowledge of both the extent and depth of technical communication, and second, by providing early technical documents for stylistic analyses which sometimes can be tied to known outcomes such as reader response.

3. Creating the revolutionary idea that the motion of
    atomic particles is guided by some mysterious pilot
    waves, de Broglie was too slow to develop a strict
    mathematical theory of this phenomenon, and, in
    1926, about a year after his publication, there
    appeared an article by a German physicist, Erwin
    Schroedinger, who wrote a general equation for de
    Broglie waves and proved its validity for all kinds
    of electron motion.

4. It should be clear that the discussion in the
    earlier sections of this chapter brought to light
    only a small number of the ways in which the
    overall grammar is simplified by introducing
    transformations and that it is not so much that the
    negative insertion transformation provides direct
    evidence for the question transformation, or vice
    versa, for neither would be very greatly
    complicated if we failed to include the other in
    our theory, but rather that, if there were no
    transformations, the overall grammar would be very
    greatly complicated, and once we include one rule
    of this general type, then the way is open to
    include many.

28. SENTENCE COMBINING

In technical writing, sentences are more often too long than too short. But ironically, sentence combining is one of the editor's greatest weapons to nest ideas and tighten copy. Try to improve these.

1. There is a greater danger from tidal waves in
    shallow waters than in deep waters. The reason for
    this is the phenomenon of the wave crest to
    increase in height as it gets closer to shore.

2. Lasers of this type can cause serious eye injury if
    they are viewed directly; that is, if the laser
    beam, or a specularly reflected beam, enters the
    eye. A specular reflection is one produced by a
    mirror-like surface, as opposed to a diffuse
    reflection.

3. The unit is equipped with a holster that holds the
    unit when it's not being used. The holster protects
    the unit from the damage which might occur if it
    were sitting loose inside the cab. It also protects
    the driver and passenger from being struck by the
    unit in the event of an accident.

4. DMG is trying to accurately describe the earthquake
   scenario in inner and coastal regions. The purpose
   is to give earthquake planners an idea of the
   expected earthquake damage.

5. The draft facility plan should be sent to the
   clearinghouse for a second review 30 days before
   any public hearing on the plan. If there is not a
   public hearing, the draft plan should be sent to
   the clearinghouse a reasonable time before it is
   sent to the state for approval.

29. REPETITION

In technical editing, one of the main chores is to remove repetition. Improve these sentences. (Hint: Do not be overly frightened of pronouns.)

1. Each applicant should be sure that his or her name appears on each page of his or her application papers.

2. Identify defective probes and then replace probes.

3. If toner is spilled, use a vacuum to clean up the loose toner.

4. If you are using a daisy wheel printer, find the table of printable characters in the printer manual which was furnished with the printer.

5. You can center the classification above or below the table or illustration, place it within the table or illustration, or place it to either side above or below the table or illustration.

6. Although in circumstances that require exception reports in addition to the regular periodic reports, when the due dates fall within five days of one another combining an exception report with periodic report is justified.

7. Through the use of synthetic nitrogenous fertilizers, which emit nitrogen oxides into the atmosphere in the process of decomposing into the soil, farmers throughout the world added to the amount of nitrogen oxide in the air.

8. The desire to maintain language distance between ruler and ruled is another reason for the language differences in colonized and colonizer situations.

9. Growing up in an environment without these needs, people grow up automatically without realizing that their needs have not been met and are not being met.

10. Our problem here on earth is the abnormal buildup of carbon dioxide in our atmosphere, directly related to automobiles, factories, burning of forests and deforestation, coal burning, and several other small factors that add up to produce a significant amount of carbon dioxide.

11. Do not override or circumvent (defeat) the
    interlocks.

12. Extensive use of Value Engineering and Life Cycle
    Cost techniques will be utilized.

13. To specify tape and batch output requirements for
    entering data into the system, the job output
    specifications form must be used. This form was
    designed for the programmer to use in describing
    file attributes for data entry and for data entry
    personnel to use as a run sheet when outputting
    data files. The following procedure describes how
    users should fill out the job output specifications
    form.

14. Off-line: Not currently connected to or under the
    control of the computer. Used to refer to equipment
    such as printers and disk drives, information
    storage media such as disks, and the information
    they contain. Compare on-line.

    On-line: Currently connected to and under the
    control of the computer. Used to refer to equipment
    such as printers and disk drives, information
    storage media such as disks, and the information
    they contain. Compare off-line.

15. If a clock loses, say, one second per decade, its error may not be apparent at the end of a year or the end of ten.

16. From this class you can expect to gain the technical skills necessary to become an improved writer. You will get the opportunity to become a better writer.

17. Plain paper has a print side. For the best print quality print only on the print side of the plain paper. The print side is not visible to the naked eye, so before you remove the paper from a ream to use in your printer, check the label on the end of the ream. The print side will be indicated by an arrow or other symbol on the label. Remove, undisturbed from the ream, the number of sheets of paper you wish to use in your printer, and load them print-side-down into the media tray.

18. Last on the list of major depletion-causing factor created by man is anything containing tropospherically stable halocarbons that contain chlorine or bromine, both of which cause depletion of the ozone.

19. Symmetrical balance occurs when both sides of the vertical centerline consist of identical elements that are equal in weight. Asymmetrical balance consists of unidentical elements on both sides of the centerline that are equal in visual weight.

20. Corrections for field procedures are always appropriate, but the overburden correction may or may not be appropriate, depending on the procedures used by those who developed the analysis method under consideration.

21. Crews are trained to evacuate planes in case of emergency water landing quickly enough to safely evacuate everyone, so the airlines claim.

22. On-schedule production and delivery of high-quality, concise, accurate documentation which meets all requirements is vital in assuring that performance of the mission will not be impeded by lack of the necessary technical information properly documented, or by incomplete, inaccurate, or late reports and manuals.

30. DOUBLETS

Technical writing could do without so many doublets—"prepare and submit," "separately and supplementally," etc. Try to remove doublets from these passages without changing the meaning at all.

1. The broad range of techniques and processes that sometimes complicate the preparation of well-designed and effective presentation material can be more efficiently utilized by personnel who are professionally engaged in the art and have the necessary equipment and materials to do a quality job.

2. The system has several features, the most important of which is the ability to send and receive messages to and from vehicles.

3. Codependence is any suffering and/or dysfunction that is associated with or results from focusing on the needs and behavior of others.

4. Animals have a kind of value that is not the same as, and is not reducible to, and is incommensurate with their having utility relative to the interests of others.

5. The increased manufacture and use of computers in
   recent years has added many words to the English
   language, as well as abbreviating and eliminating
   many others.

6. Factors may include mild to moderate physical
   abuse, covert or less obvious mental abuse, mental
   and emotional abuse, child neglect, and ignoring or
   thwarting of the child's spirituality or spiritual
   growth.

7. The atmosphere is constantly in flux, moving and
   changing in temperature, density, and pressure,
   depending on the sun, location, altitude, and
   surface differences.

8. The characteristic pits of woody elements are often
   preserved and also signify vascular plants derived
   from a terrestrial, or land-based, environment.

9. One of the major objectives of the program is to
   support state and local efforts to implement
   comprehensive community-based drunk driving
   programs and to improve countermeasure
   effectiveness and efficiency within such programs.

10. A greater willingness is needed on the part of
    society in general to provide adequate and
    appropriate care and treatment to all those who
    fall into the wide spectrum of the mentally ill.

11. Ozone is one thing that needs to be studied,
    preserved, and, if possible, slowly restored to
    levels estimated to exist before the industrial
    revolution.

12. Pregnant health workers should be especially
    familiar with and strictly adhere to the universal
    precautions.

13. This is a dynamic documentation effort; as each new
    phase or area of the program is tested and
    completed or modified, the appropriate
    documentation is updated or newly produced.

14. Several different engineers, analysts, or
    programmers may contribute to the same report or
    document while having widely varying writing styles
    or philosophies as to the amount of technical
    detail or to the approach they take in documenting
    their efforts.

15. Time constraints and document production schedules,
    when first imposed, may have been reasonable, but
    with confrontation of such things as increased task
    scope, better understanding of the details involved
    as the effort progresses, and unforeseen technical
    problems requiring more depth of documentation,
    they may necessitate an accelerated document
    production effort to meet schedules or to avoid
    delaying follow-on tasks.

31. CUT UNNECESSARY WORDS

1. Accounting is one of the largest fields of
   professional employment, with almost a half-milli⦊
   people working in this occupation.

2. The onboard computer is responsible for
   accomplishing all autopilot, navigation, guidance,
   and flight sequencing functions.

3. Tests showed their circumferential tensile strengt⦊
   to be approximately 40,000 psi, well above the
   level required for long range missile applications

4. Like all successful jobs, adequate decisions of th⦊
   right kind at the right time were made to ensure
   that the critical performance within the time
   factor was possible.

5. This program benefits people in that it will
   improve technical writing skills in the areas of
   resumes, proposals, manuals, and communication wit⦊
   others.

6. In the document shown on the screen, move the
   cursor back two spaces, using the left-arrow key.

7. References should be included in the paper sufficient to enable the reader to acquire additional information should she desire.

8. Most shops don't charge for labor, but unfortunately profit by tacking a healthy markup on the oil and filter.

9. It is impractical and moreover impossible to design a structure that will survive all possible worst-case scenarios.

10. Typically, the bigger the operation and the more extensive the changes, the more devastating the negative results can be.

11. Once you set the switches, you will not need to reset them unless you change your system so that it requires a different configuration.

12. The degree of periorbital edema often provides some clue as to what is happening intracranially in terms of swelling.

13. The total amount of the loan was six million dollars.

14. These things, though of a useful character, were not what he wanted.

15. These statistics serve to show the effects of inadequate supervision.

16. We made an error and failed to credit your payment.

17. There are some products that have more eye appeal.

18. The book is divided into various sections, all dealing with the matter of employment.

19. Familiarity with the methods whereby printing operations can be performed is highly beneficial.

20. There is a possibility that some of the employees may be late because of the fact that busses are not running.

21. The field of economics is one in which computer
    studies have often been used successfully.

22. The developing of methods of training dogs in
    obedience has posed quite a problem for dog owners
    for years.

23. To obtain the best possible results in the
    application of desktop publishing it is sometimes
    to modify the procedures for using the software in
    order to suit the characteristics and practical
    requirements of particular users.

24. The apparent extension of the field' s propagation
    will be dependent upon the discernment sensitivity
    of the instrumentation.

25. The effects of gaseous composition on the
    determination of convective heating rates is known
    to a comparatively high degree.

26. Also shown is an estimate of the percentage of
    total personnel effort to be devoted to each of the
    major tasks as a function of the time period.

27. Consideration will be given to advertising
effectiveness to a degree consistent with the
definition of costs expended.

28. Software incompatibility and personnel inexperience
will be accounted for during the phases where these
effects are significant.

29. A test plan will be defined for obtaining the
medical data which is not presently available but
which is necessary in order to utilize the each of
the pharmaceuticals on elderly populations.

30. A verification philosophy will be selected and the
procedures and equipment required to implement the
selected philosophy will be specified.

31. The planned approach for definition of the new and/
or modified operating requirements identified above
is essentially as outlined above.

32. Overall system performance will be specified to the
extent possible in terms of system accuracy over a
specified range of terrain types, weather
conditions, and periphery equipment noise
contributions.

33. To enter the competition submit a completed entry form.

34. A tunnel has been built and is currently in operation.

35. Figure 6-1 provides an illustration of the cable.

36. To receive a copy of the survey results, write the editor.

37. Adults become ready to learn when they experience in their life situation a need to know or a need to be able to do something in order to perform more effectively and satisfyingly.

38. The fact of the matter is that the office does not have enough time in its allotment to make expenditures on programs of this nature.

39. Our findings argue persuasively that although a
    high degree of ability as measured by the
    achievement test may be required for attainment of
    a doctorate, given the nature of graduate
    education, these ability measures account for only
    a small percentage of the variations in job
    performance measurements.

40. Those maintaining that such tight bureaucratic
    regulation is necessary to stabilize both prices
    and production should be the most diligent in
    support of the development and utilization of all
    forms or organizations and of procedures available
    for peaceful resolution of the conflict between the
    various segments of the industry, such as
    arbitration and conciliation.

2. ADD WORDS

Sometimes editors have to add words for clarity. Try improving these sentences.

1. Document the procedures, complications, age, and
   distal pulses.

2. Since 80% of jobs are found indirectly, begin
   networking when you are not seeking a position.

3. We propose 1) a surface-floating bridge or 2) an
   underwater bridge suspended from the ocean bottom.

33. SEQUENCE

Sometimes an editor can make a tremendous difference with very small touches, even moving a single small word or phrase. See if you can find the key that improves the sequence in these sentences.

1. A 30 in. by 30 in. cutaway may be very effective,
   but if it is reduced to a 2 in. by 2 in. square in
   its published form in a repair manual, it does not
   communicate.

2. VEU Industries officially launched a project that
   will add to its technology base in the rapidly
   expanding field of numerically controlled machining
   operations May 28.

3. Technical writers are there to help new and
   seasoned consultants alike to more effectively
   practice their trade.

4. Society members as well as non-members are invited
   to attend the next meeting.

5. Technology transfer is the subject of a
   presentation that Joseph Brown will give.

6. Inadequacies in contingency plans or severely
   underestimating the ultimate costs to the consumer
   can be disastrous.

4. USELESS CATEGORIES

Wordy writers often have trouble coming straight to the point and insert an extra phrase
to categorize their topic. Pick out the useless category names in the following examples.

1. The purpose of this letter is to give high praise
    to our sales staff for the excellent January
    results.

    Our sales staff deserves high praise for its
    excellent January results.

2. A feature of our employee benefit program, which
    ranks with the best in industry, is the opportunity
    to earn advanced degrees at company expense.

3. What this particular piece of machinery is is a
    precursor of the combine.

4. The trouble with that hypothesis is that it fails
    to account for all the observed motions.

5. Although in most instances of zinc-bearing ores in
    the region of the Upper Congo it is the case that
    they occur in conjunction with the ores of other
    metals, in the Ntagwe district they do not.

6. The following is a list of graphic software which
    is highly recommended and appropriate for use in a
    technical report.

7. The main usage of this manual is as an aid in
    preparing your documents to be helpful to the user.

8. Newsletters are evaluated by a panel of judges in
    these areas: essential elements, such as newsletter
    size, frequency, and title; recommended topics,
    such as meeting notices and reports, feature
    articles, and chapter activities; editorial
    quality, such as usage, style, and impression; and
    design and production, such as page design and
    production.

9. As the neurological picture is greatly influenced
    by the degree of cerebral edema and resultant
    increase in intracranial pressure, numerous medical
    and nursing interventions employed in the
    postoperative period are aimed at minimizing these
    reactions.

35. METADISCOURSE

A common fault in technical writing is what Joseph M. Williams* calls "metadiscourse," or addressing the audience about one's own concerns rather than about the subject. This is most common in software manuals that discuss the manual before the software.) Edit these sentences, if you can.

1. It seems clear that it is common for it to become
   cloudy when it rains.

2. Since the significance of system reconfiguration is
   often overlooked with regard to memory-related
   problems, this chapter presents a rather detailed
   examination of the computer's memory system before
   discussing the actual problems that may occur. The
   fact that most changes in memory capacity will
   create an apparent system error during POST, until
   the PC is properly reconfigured, is the reason for
   presenting this information.

---

*See *Style: Ten Lessons in Clarity and Grace,* 4th ed. (New York: Harper Collins, 1994), pp. 79–81.

36. THE EDITOR AS A HEDGE TRIMMER

Editors owe it to their readership and project budgets to try to make their publication as efficient as they can, while making them friendly to their readers. This means being direct, clear, and straightforward. In this exercise, explain how you would deal sympathetically with authors who feel it their duty to hedge.

1. It is important to note that in the application of the theory to particular situations, it may be necessary in many cases to make adjustments to compensate for exogenous factors.

2. To listen to and analyze successive groups of supervisors diagnose, discuss, and attempt to resolve their communication problems inevitably leads to the consideration of whether many or most of what we call communication problems (and perceive as such) might not only be symptoms of other difficulties which exist between persons and groups.

7. FAULTY STRUCTURE

tructure may be the single most important concept in technical editing, partly because e structure of some writing is so poor. Do what you can to bandage these victims.

1. The valve configuration that was finally decided upon was to use a pneumatically operated valve, solenoid controlled, and the valve element itself was a ball type.

2. Technical writing helps substantiate or perhaps organize results of research findings and to market programs.

3. At a height of approximately 25 kilometers, ozone is the most concentrated, but it can be detected as high as 50 kilometers.

4. Wipe the bottle opening with the napkin to remove any excess cork or lead from the protective covering.

5. Ensure a planned route for moving the system to its operating location is confirmed by checking overhead, side, and corner turn clearances and that all necessary facilities are available for the unobstructed passage of the system along the planned route.

6. The group included one man who had installed
   himself in a plastic bag in Central Park, sharing
   it on winter nights with some of the park's
   aggressive rat packs and a foul-mouthed blind woma
   who defended her home turf with an unending stream
   of epithets.

7. Driven by the creation of a new society, the growt
   of urban areas and their relation to jobs, cities,
   and economic expansion, the Industrial Revolution
   began an era of unprecedented advances, but at the
   cost of harming one major resource, the earth.

8. With the hole in the ozone over Antarctica allowin
   more ultraviolet radiation to reach the surface of
   the earth, photoplankton, a simple lifeform, is
   threatened, which threatens the base for all life,
   be it aquatic or terrestrial, in that region.
   Providing us with a glimpse of the future, the rol
   that photoplankton has in the fabric of life and
   its potential devastation could be a sign of futur
   changes to come for the earth.

9. The documentation of unwanted sexual activity
   reported in 1993 found 7.8% of 858 women admitted
   previous experience of unwanted sexual activity
   when admitted to a university's student health car
   facility for a routine gynecological exam.

10. In trying to bring the best to local businesses and homeowners, please take a moment and fill out the enclosed Health and Fitness questionnaire and when completed please return in the signed envelope provided.

11. Technical writing is an integral part not only in engineering communication but the entire profession.

38. DECIDE WHAT ELSE IS NOT NEEDED

Editing tips cannot cover all cases. Try your hand at the following sentences, usin
your own good ideas to interest the reader.

1. Our plan includes separation of application
    software from physical data access and storage
    considerations so as to enable the installation an(
    production use of software developments produced b
    the Integrated Sheet Metal Center (ISMC) and the
    Advanced Machining System (AMS) and application
    software produced by other companies or outside
    software houses as it becomes available and as we
    extend our implementations throughout the factory.

    **As we extend our own implementations throughout
    the factory, we plan to segregate the software
    developed by our Integrated Sheet Metal Center
    (ISMC) and Advanced Machining System (AMS) from
    that produced outside.**

2. In communications theory, superfluous information
    is called "noise"; these sources of unclarity are
    "noise" sources. They are "semantic noise" sources
    a noise of meaning (to be distinguished from
    "engineering noise" such as static and transient
    waves from equipment and the medium).

3. The impact of negative slides on visibility and
    viewer attention is clearly positive.

4. As the technology expands, the reduced cost of
    computer memory, processing, and available mass-
    produced technology will likely reduce costs.

5. Due to the overwhelming amount of information
    available to the user today, it is beneficial to
    know where to begin. Once this is accomplished, it
    is essential to note the multitude of products
    available, along with the capabilities and costs,
    in an effort to relieve an anxiety experience by
    those who are misinformed, or who are relatively
    new to the field of computer graphics.

6. From the state of contemporary astronomy a man
    without Copernicus' Neoplatonic bias might have
    concluded merely that the problem of the planets
    could have no solution that was simultaneously
    simple and precise.

39. INFERRING MEANING FROM SYNTACTIC CLUES

Do any of the following sentences seem to need restructuring? Does the glossary on page 87 help you restructure them?

1. Clausteriggled permagloze will maklerate multifrangible monopigsimules whenever a zygoplam trigloptrerizes each of a set of demonuperted tragloglumps.

2. A zygoplam will trigloptrerize each of a set of demonuperted tragloglumps whenever a researcher maklerates multifrangible monopigsimules with clausteriggled permagloze.

3. Multifrangible monopigsimules are maklerated by clausteriggled permagloze whenever each of a set of demonuperted tragloglumps is trigloptrerized by a zygoplam.

4. By maklerating multifrangible monopigsimules with clausteriggled permagloze, the researcher can cause a zygoplam to trigloptrerize each of a set of demonuperted tragloglumps.

5. Permagloze, having been clausteriggled, will create makleration of multifrangible monopigsimules, provided that trigloptrerization by zygoplammatic action has affected a set of demonuperted tragloglumps.

6. Whenever each of a set of demonuperted tragloglumps is trogloptrerized by an ygoplam, the consequence is multifrangibled monopigsimuled makleration, provided that clausteriggled permagloze is introduced.

7. Provided that demonuperted tragloglumps have been trigloptrerized by a zygoplam, one can predict that multifrangible monopigsimules will be maklerated by permagloze previously clausteriggled.

8. The prediction of the occurrence of multifrangible monopigsimulated makleration by the action of clausteriggled permagloze will be more confident if trigloptrerization by zygoplammatic action of a set of demonuperted tragloglumps occurs.

Even editors who lack degrees in science can nevertheless edit technical prose successfully. Why? Because they infer from syntactic clues the relations among concepts, then restructure the syntax to express the relations more clearly. From the syntax, figure out which of the following statements are inconsistent with the others.

9. When the frammis of an ognivator becomes fribbled, the riplogle of the zyfling birklet is likely to glirpen.

10. A shurf kleb will fribble the frammis of an ognivator. When fribbled, the frammis may cause glirpenation of the riplogle of the zyfling birklet.

11. An ognivator whose frammis is fribbled may glirpen
    the zyfling birklet's riplogle.

12. Fribbling an ognivator's frammis, in most casess,
    glirpens the birklet's riplogle, genurfing the
    birklet from zyfling.

13. Zyfling, the priggle zumat of birklets, may be
    genurfed if an ognivator's frammis has become
    fribbled, thus glirpening its riplogle.

14. When a riplogle glirpens, as may jengur if the
    ognivator's frammis becomes fribbled, the birklet
    can no longer zyfle.

15. The jenguration of the fribbling of an ognivator's
    frammis genurfs the zyflation of the birklet.

GLOSSARY FOR EXERCISE 39

Clausteriggle—to cause a clauster to become iggled, as in "clausteriggled permagloze."

Demonuperted—when a singular pert becomes decentrifupled in combination with especially any of a set of traglophytes.

Maklerate—to create makleration reactions, esp. of monopigsimules; to mipanulize duopigsimules into mono states.

Minipigsimule—the opposite of monopigsimule (which see). Not to be confused with threelittlepigsimule, a Walt Disney aberration.

Monopigsimule—one of a class of pigsimules characterized by identity dissomulation; opposed to minipigsimule (which see). Usually involved in the process of makleration.

Permagloze—a hypermetallic non-ionic-bondable stropclase often found associated with haphazardites and glissomates. Soluble in dichlorethylabase-diphenyloxyparabenzenecandidoftentate.

Tragloglump—a genus of the class traraglophytus directus, occurring only in south-western Africa in the interferules of subterranean geoclynes. Sometimes used in its purified state in laboratory experiments with trigloptrerization processes.

Trigloptrerize—as an elaborate three-step process, used to alter the reaction of a zygoplam, especially in the makleration of monopigsimules.

Zygoplam—a heterated publicondria (*Heterata publicondrichondria*) which, when reduced to its pertiplate state, will coagulate intragalactically in the trigloptrerization process, producing zygoplastic residues useful, in combination with stearated oglivine, to regulate the panformdigeling of extrapyramidal fructose.

Thanks to the late Dr. Lee Garner, who directed the technical writing group at Sandia National Laboratories. Dr. Garner used the preceding sentences and glossary to show that unfamiliar vocabulary need not deter editors from changing the structure of awkward sentences.

40. EDITING POMPOSITY

Some technical writing is so pompous it's difficult to read. See if you can make Sentence No. 2 more friendly.

1. Following completion of the interview, the entire
    form should be forwarded to the appropriate
    department and/or subdivision head for their
    evaluation and approval. Please return the subject
    forms to the appropriate personnel divisional
    office by 11 June.

    **After you complete the interview, please fill out
    the form, have it evaluated by the department or
    subdivision head, and return it to Personnel by
    June 11.**

2. Input from the customer concerning media
    applicability will be a factor that determines a
    set of methods/media plans to be considered for
    training customer personnel.

Explain why the following passage may be ineffective. Circle and number the phrasings you identify and key them by number to your discussions. Then express this concept more economically.

3. One of the most crucial and important questions
    that must be faced by each and every one of us is
    the question of whether or not a continuation of
    existence in its current form, involving a passive
    acquiescence in the eventualities imposed on us
    from external sources, is to be preferred over the
    alternative of making an attempt to mount an
    opposition to the seeming exigencies of these
    externalities with the intention of effectuating
    their termination.

41. THE IRISH BULL

"The Irish Bull originates in the imaginative power of the Irish people. It proceeds from a superabundance of ideas, which crowd one another so fast in an Irishman's brain that they get jammed together in the doorway of his speech and can only tumble out in their ordinary disorder. It is always comprehensible, even when it is most confused." (*Bulls and Blunders*, ed. Marshall Brown. Chicago: S.C. Griggs, 1893.)

Make these sentences more precise.

1. I came around to see you and there you were, gone.

2. The only way to prevent what is past is to put a stop to it before it happens.

3. In one year there were 580,000 cases where handguns were used, including minor assaults in which the gun was not used.

4. One behavior that is very effective is to refuse to ride with someone who is known to get drunk and not accept it.

5. Start/stop timer button: The name of this button is what it can do for many functions.

6. The emissions from supersonic transport planes eject nitrogen oxides into the stratosphere.

7. Information on changing the battery will not be mentioned here, so please note the caution and recommendation for the replacement of the battery.

8. In a reducing environment, carbonaceous microfossils may last indefinitely.

9. A small percentage of the amount of depletion the ozone suffers can be earmarked by the space shuttle ironically in that the shuttle has done a vast amount of research regarding the study of our atmosphere.

10. Growing up in an environment without these needs, people grow up automatically without realizing that their needs have not been met and are not being met.

11. His writing skills are not the greatest and any sort of help in this area is worth it.

12. Plugs shall be so designed that it is impossible to insert a wrong plug into a receptacle whenever the possibility exists.

13. I have little knowledge in technical writing other than creative and expository writing.

42. ZEUGMA (FALSE PARALLELISM)

Rephrase these sentences to remove the sometimes unintended humor.

1. He took his hat, his coat, and his leave.

2. He left in low gear and high dudgeon.

3. "Probably there had never been such a mingling of art, sex, politics, spiritualism, cold meats, and lettuce sandwiches." (Oscar Cargill, on the "evenings" of Mabel Luhan early in the 1900's in New York.)

4. Rotary presses use shorter times and longer paper.

5. Using computer graphics, images can be enhanced, moved, criticized, and enlarged.

6. Although the cost of separating a single job by computer can run as high as $1000, it is produced in one-tenth the time and accuracy of the same job done manually.

7. Your sales representative is familiar with your
    needs, equipment, and software and should be able
    to help you.

8. Typically, the only way one finds out about the
    unadvertised costs and the horror stories is by
    word of mouth.

9. A good user manual should be researched thoroughly,
    indexed exhaustively, and easy to navigate through.

LESSON

4

Now that you've become adept at fixing problems in sentences, try the following exercises to make sentences work together coherently and emphatically.

Improving Paragraphs

43. REORGANIZE PARAGRAPHS USING THE INCHWORM CONCEPT

A corollary of the theme-rheme idea is the inchworm concept (see Chapter 6, pp. 61–62), in which you start one sentence where another leaves off. Rearrange these sentences to make such connections.

1. Silicon is the second most abundant element on the earth's crust. Sand is made primarily of silicon.

2. The exposed side must have a minimum amount of metal, to maximize solar absorption. As you reduce the metal, junction resistance increases. This will lower your power.

3. The struggle to define the unique qualities of technical writing began considerably earlier. Royal Society members made the decision to promote a "plain" style during the scientific revolution of the seventeenth century. Flowery language and convoluted sentence structure were deemed inappropriate.

4. We must understand who initiates efforts to promote water conservation before we can understand how a community makes decisions about environmental issues. Agencies who have been designated to plan and manage water quality have initiated such efforts. They have also helped volunteer groups begin efforts, offering technical advice and assistance in coordinating their activities.

5. Sodium, potassium, and calcium (among other things)
    in a solution in about the proportions found in
    frogs' blood can keep a frog's heart alive and
    beating outside its body. Each mineral is somehow
    essential for functioning of the muscle. The
    solution is called Ringer's solution. It is named
    after the English physician Sidney Ringer, who made
    this discovery in 1882.

6. I soon began to make a list of problems in
    technical writing. My own assignments were
    frequently the source of these problems. My first
    effort was returned with the "doublets" circled
    in red.

44. KEEP THE TOPIC FORWARD

Besides inchworming, the other main technique for helping readers follow paragraphs is keeping the topic in view. To keep a topic forward, make it the subject of most of a paragraph's sentences or allude to it near the front of most sentences. Reorganize these paragraphs to keep the topic in view.

1. Some Scud attacks came frighteningly close. Tom
    Stanley and other field reps were gathered in their
    office in Dhahran when the building shook from the
    nearby impact of a Scud. Stanley had just gotten
    off the phone after wishing his son back in Texas a
    happy eighth birthday when the Scud came in. "It
    just rocked this place," he recalls. The Scud had
    hit a military barracks just a block away, killing
    28 Americans.

    Some <u>Scud attacks</u> came frighteningly close. <u>One of</u>
    <u>them</u> hit a military barracks just a block away from
    Tom Stanley's office in Dhahran, killing 28
    Americans. When <u>it</u> came in, Stanley, had just
    gotten off the phone after wishing his son back in
    Texas a happy eighth birthday. "<u>It</u> just rocked this
    place," he recalls.

2. The most elusive creatures of all, willful humans,
    are the subjects of economists' researches. As the
    threshold into the world of computers was crossed,
    the possibility of collecting, organizing, and
    manipulating information on a scale previously
    unimagined was slowly realized. This made it
    possible to analyze economic phenomena that had
    previously seemed governed by chance.

3. A special study of the classification of lymphocyte
    subtypes and their radiation sensitivity was made
    on 18 former plutonium workers. Elevated T-cell
    helper/suppressor ratios were skewed to higher
    ratios for these subjects compared to 14 age-
    matched controls.

4. Older program languages continue to change as
    computing environments change. This is sometimes
    obscured by all the attention given in the press to
    object-oriented languages. In particular, Fortran
    is going through a growth spurt. Demand for a
    better Fortran has been fueled by this growth in
    Fortran-based applications. A joint ANSI-ISO
    committee has brought forth a new Fortran standard,
    Fortran 90.

5. Studies of academic writing using prompting
    programs may have limited relevance to technical
    writers. For example, students are asked by the
    academic prompting programs to explore a topic
    about which they have considerable control. These
    students are able to decide both the details of
    their topic and their approach to it. Technical
    writers, on the other hand, often find themselves
    with predefined topics and document formats. A
    fruitful application of prompting programs in
    technical writing may be in developing outlines for
    routine tasks. Several authors report success with
    field-specific computer programs that prompt novice
    writers for information necessary for structured
    documents. Perhaps prompting programs are more
    successful when their goal is limited and clearly
    specified.

45. READER IMPACT, UNITY, COHERENCE

Edit the paragraph below for reader impact, unity, and coherence, using the following tips:

Reader Impact
- Does the paragraph begin with a succinct statement of the single most important thought?
- Does the most important information appear either at the beginning or the end?

Unity
- Are related ideas grouped together?
- Does the paragraph develop only one main idea?

Coherence
- Do sentences progress like an inchworm—each starting where the previous one stopped? If not, do the sentences have the same topic?
- Are transitional words used to relate the sentences? These might include:
  Enumeration—*first, second, third, last, finally*
  Addition—*also, moreover, in addition, likewise*
  Opposition—*however, on the other hand, still, by contrast*
  Cause and effect—*therefore, thus, consequently, as a result*

It would be possible for Acme not to finance the dealers. This would reduce expenditures by approximately $1 million per year. This approach might reduce capital commitments. It would make dealers hard to come by. It would in all probability reduce sales. Dealers would not have enough equipment to produce a variety of structures. The sales necessary to produce a 15 percent return without the expense and revenue from financing the dealers were calculated. The sales resulting from this calculation were 16 percent lower than those shown in Table 1.

46. MULTIPLE PROBLEMS

This paragraph may work better if you supply an agent—say, "eye surgeons."

1. It has been stated that the assessment of the

    mobility of the detached retina is a factor when

    the nondrainage retinal detachment operation of

    Custodis and Lincoff is being given consideration.

    Determination of the mobility of the detached

    retina is made on the basis of two factors. The

    depth of the subretinal fluid is the first to be

    given consideration. If the subretinal fluid is

    shallow, then little room is given for actual

    movement of the detached retina. The longitudinal

    extent of the retinal separation is the second to

    be given consideration. On the basis of a

    determination that the depth of fluid is shallow

    (<10 mm) and the longitudinal retinal separation

    extent is in excess of 1.5 mm, it will probably be

    decided that Custodis-Lincoff is contraindicated.

In revising this passage, don't let the simple errors distract you from the more serious problems.

2. The principal question is why social systems evolve

   at all, why should their be an evolution from tribe

   to chiefdom to state; most particularly why should

   individual households agree to abide by a social

   contract with other households in which their

   surplus time is put to work or appropriate by other

   households. One author's judgement is that the

   explanation has been in terms of rising population

   densities. Included in this argument is the idea

   that social integration is closely related to the

   technology of communication and transportation.

   Following this argument, for each technological

   level of communication or transportation there is a

   practical limit to effective social integration in

   terms of the size of the territory integrated;

   hence the only way more people can be incorporated

into a social system is by increasing the number of people per square mile.

This, however, leaves unexplained the question as to why, as population per unit of space increases, we do not have simply social fission, that is more societies of the same size, why larger social systems. In our judgment, this is the crux of the problem and one to which this paper addresses itself.

3. MERIT PROMOTION PROGRAM

Two major changes over the earlier program have been effected in making merit promotion selections. The underwriting and supervisory judgment tests have been discontinued as a requirement for promotion or as a device for ranking candidates. The second change is a new supervisory evaluation system to replace the earlier employee appraisal; the new supervisory evaluation document (the Job Factor Profile) eliminates the use of total numerical scores and substitutes for it selection-screening on the basis of job factors. In the judgment of the inspectors, the Job Factor Profile permits a desirably precise evaluation of employees through a scale of nine degrees of merit in ascending order of importance covering elements appropriate to different kinds of positions.

4. LIGHTING FIXTURE LAMPS

A form No. 94-5932 without fiscal data or prices was submitted to your office on June 18 for lighting fixture lamps for the Wichita office building. These lamps have not been purchased because, at this office's request on the requisition, procurement was to await the awarding of the contract for the lighting fixtures requested on No. 94-5932.

Now that the Coleman Company has been awarded the contract for the lighting fixtures, the procurement of lamps for the fixtures can be effected. However, lamps in addition to those listed on No. 94-5732 are now required. The following list consolidates our requirements for lamps for subject project by including the

lamps listed on No. 94-5732 with the additional lamps

now required. The cost of all the lamps on this list

is chargeable to the accounting symbols appearing on

the X-200 authorization dated September 1, for $50,000

that was given to Mrs. Apple on September 30.

47. DETAIL

Detail in technical writing is highly prized. But sometimes technical writing can be so tutorial and on such a low level of abstraction that it loses the reader. It's up to the technical editor to bridge that gap. Try these sentences. Imagine circumstances where such detail by an author would be desirable.

1. Check YES if all physical records (blocks) must be the same length. Check NO if the block requirement is a multiple of the logical record length. This will indicate that padding is not required.

    Check YES if padding is required in order to make all blocks the same length. Otherwise check NO.

2. A pair of electromagnetic coils is mounted behind each hammer and wound around each pole piece. The coils are normally de-energized. When hammer drive logic determines that the hammer must print a dot, a current pulse energizes the coils. The polarity of the resulting magnetic field opposes the field of the permanent magnet, cancelling its effect and releasing the hammer. The hammer springs forward, strikes the ribbon and paper, and leaves a dot impression of the hammer tip on the paper.

3. Fire, to a chemist, is part of a more general
   process called oxidation. This occurs whenever
   excess oxygen combines with elements having a
   positive valence.

4. If you have in fact filed your quarterly tax, there
   should be a record of it in the database of the
   regional IRS office.

48. PRECISION

Technical editing requires precision. See if you can make these passages more precise. One trick is to use the active voice.

1. Forests have a large percentage of living biomass, though a proportionately smaller part of the productivity. Tree trunks in a forest don't exchange carbon to any great degree, but the leaves do. Proportionately more of the trees are biomass but don't exchange much carbon. In a savannah you'll see that ratio of biomass to productivity is smaller than in forests.

2. The potential for ground damage that a small plane can cause is much smaller as compared to commercial airliners on land.

3. Carbon dioxide is a main factor in the function of the greenhouse effect, the process which helps trap the incoming solar radiation from the sun in order to keep the earth warm.

4. It was discovered by Osburn and Peters that
    emulsification of fibrous nodular masses is
    facilitated by a topical application of a lysin
    substance.

5. Because of the instruments used in calculating the
    approximate amounts of ozone over Antarctica in
    previous years, scientists were unable to identify
    the hole.

LESSON

5

Improving Longer Documents

The most rewarding part of an editor's job is acting as a "beta tester" for the readers. In that role, you have to think about who the readers will be—their backgrounds, their interests, their tolerance for reading. You have to think about what the document is supposed to accomplish. Then you have to decide whether the information in the draft is adequate: Is anything important missing? Is there too much detail? What is the best format for this purpose and this audience?

9. EDIT SUMMARY

Edit this summary to reduce wordiness. Consider paragraphing.

Among the persons interviewed, there was an expressed interest, and an indicated need, for additional training that would better equip supervisors to counsel, motivate, and where appropriate, to constructively discipline workers. Additional details relating to this need appear elsewhere in this report, in the section "Employee and Supervisory Effectiveness." A number of the complaints made in interviews voiced the feeling that non-merit discrimination is sometimes involved in the selection of persons to be given tryouts or on-the-job training in assignments that improve opportunities for advancement.

50. EDIT SHORT REPORT

Edit the following survey report, addressed to management. Consider paragraphing. Then use the same information to announce a new, automated system to employees.

TRAINING SURVEY

The current procedures for accomplishment of the annual training survey have some operational weaknesses that should be strengthened. Presently, the Personnel and Training Division is given only the total numerical needs for planned courses by the reporting office. There are no names submitted to the P&T Division as to the employees who need the training, although Area, Branch, and Regional Divisional training co-ordinators obtain this information. This results in an automatic assumption that stated numerical needs are valid. There is no indication that an effort is being made to relate reported need to the proposed training identified on employee appraisal forms, or to utilize the date for establishment of training priorities with the Region or specific organizations. It is anticipated that by the year 2000 an automated system will be available

which will show the kind of training each individual
has had, as well as an outline of the courses needed.
Implementation of the new system should improve the
annual needs survey and update the individual training
record card index; however, the Region will still have
to consider establishment of priorities for both
nominated employees and requested courses.

51. EDIT SHORT ARTICLE

COMPUTERS IN DESIGN AND PRINTING

Recent advances have opened up a new world of art,
design, and visual applications for computers.
Computer graphics have expanded for use
in engineering, drafting, charts and graphs for
reports, and slides for speakers.

The advantages for using computers in design are
clearly positive. Computers provide the link between
problems and their solutions with visible
alternatives, in a shorter amount of time. Computer
graphics can reduce turnaround time for problem
solving and cut costs for problem solutions. On a
satellite run of a U.S. military program, the problem
occurred in analyzing returning satellite data.
Without computer graphics it took one month to get
calculations done to obtain a result. In 48 hours it
can be done by graphics.

The benefits of using computer graphics involve
productivity, creativity, and speed. Sophisticated

computer programs are now prohibitively expensive. As the technology expands the reduced cost of computer memory, processing, and available mass produced technology will likely reduce costs.

Images can be enhanced, moved, enlarged, etc., once created, relieving users of repetitive design tasks. This is producing more. Costly mistakes can be reduced since design alternatives are efficiently viewed and the most pleasing design chosen. You can view trial and error designs in a fraction of the time to see them by conventional means.

One of the fields already using computer graphics is graphic arts and printing. In print shops, newspapers, and magazines, most typesetting today is done by means of phototypesetting, replacing the old hot lead type. The typesetter uses a computer to set type in magazines, books, and ad copy.

Computers are being used to control presses. Making it possible to adjust colors on massive runs, particularly in newspaper printing. It can automate manual operations, thus increasing staff productivity.

Computers can refine and manipulate images, create

finished artwork from initial roughs.

The fastest area of growth for printing firms is in

color separation by computer. One of the firms is

Microtype, Inc., using this extensively. Although the

cost of separating a single job can run as high as

$1000, it is produced in one-tenth the time and

accuracy of the same job done manually.

52. WHAT DO READERS REALLY NEED TO KNOW?

Here's the draft of a one-sheet manual. It will be packed inside a box along with the product, which is fully assembled. Consider how much of the information presented here will actually be useful to readers and cut out the rest. Then lay out the document so that buyers will easily find essential information.

The hand-operated airpump is designed for inflating bicycle tires and sporting goods such as basketballs, footballs, and lightweight rubber rafts. It is compact, lightweight, and portable. It is rated at 60 psi (pounds per square inch). The rustproof steel construction will give many years of useful service.

The airpump consists of three main parts: the barrel assembly, the plunger assembly, and the hose. The pump is 18½ inches high and is constructed of steel. It has rubber hosing and brass fittings.

The barrel assembly consists of three subparts: housing, barrel cap, and toeplate. The housing is a hollow 2½-inch by 17-inch steel barrel. The top is threaded to receive the barrel cap. The octagonal brass barrel cap allows access to the pump mechanism's diaphragm. It is threaded to attach to the housing and has a 1/4-inch hole in its center to slide over the

shaft. A 1/8-inch hole in the side of the cap allows
air to enter the housing. Welded to the bottom of the
barrel housing is a 4½-inch long toeplate on which the
operator stands while operating the pump's plunger
mechanism.

The plunger assembly consists of three subparts: a
rod, a handle, and a diaphragm. The plunger assembly
fits into the housing, secured by the barrel cap. The
rod is a 1/4-inch by 16½-inch steel shaft, threaded at
both ends. A 6-inch wooden handle threads onto the top
of the rod. A diaphragm, a leather washer, is secured
to the lower end of the rod by two
1/4-inch nuts, one on either side.

The 18-inch fabric-covered hose screws into the
barrel housing one. The locking clamp nozzle is
inserted into the hose end and is secured with a 1/8-
inch metal band. A thumb chuck allows quick release
for regular and high-pressure use.

The operator clamps the hose nozzle onto the filler
stem of the tire to be inflated, stands on the toe

plate, and pumps the plunger up and down to inflate the tire with air. If the item to be inflated is a sporting good, the supplied filler needle is first inserted into the nozzle clamp.

53. EDIT JOB DESCRIPTION

Rewrite this job description, but don't try to assign a title to the job. Also, don't use the decimal numbers and don't bother to attach names to all the acronyms.

1.   In order to carry out management's program, hardware status and program control are the primary concern of the writer, involving the following duties.

1.1   Review, and incorporation into weekly status reports, of vendor and in-house assembly and review progress, versus planning need dates.

1.1.1 Analysis of effects on master schedule; when significantly affected, seek corrective action with Systems Manager or Production Control.

1.2   The writer is responsible for the Aircraft Fuel System and associated tankage, tubes, and fittings. To control them, he has to:

1.2.1 Originate and maintain system hardware status by aircraft of serial numbers and delivery dates of various part numbers involved.

1.3   To keep up with daily efforts of other groups affecting project status, it is necessary to review and analyze the following reaching writer's desk.

1.3.1 Buyers' and Engineers' ACIEs and Purchase Order Changes.

1.3.2   Hardware test failures, MRRs, Failure Analysis,
        Lab and Qualification Test reports.

1.3.3   Manufacturing schedule progress reports,
        Production and Spares Support shortage lists,
        Procurement Requests, ECPs, and Air Force
        changes.

1.3.4   Drawing up charts and graphs for management and
        Air Force changes.

1.4   In volatile systems, as the writer has, many
        repairs, retrofits, and design changes are
        required for optimum performance; this entails
        monitoring of following:

1.4.1   Contacting vendors daily on outstanding
        shortages for progress and shipping dates.

1.4.2   Allocating and shifting hardware to overcome
        shortages, adjusting assembly dates, and
        expediting where possible.

1.4.3   Field trips, reports, and memos to accomplish
        the above, as well as written recommendations
        on various proposals, are made by the writer.

1.4.4   Close liaison with Engineering Procurement,
        Reliability, and Production Control is
        maintained. It is necessary to review and
        analyze many of their technical reports in
        order to get needed information.

54. EDIT USER MANUAL

Assume you have been contracted by an Asian firm to improve the following instruc
tions. Revise them, then produce a letter to the client explaining the changes.

TO THE ATTENTION OF THE IONIZER'S USER

Dear User,

Please read the following information carefully:

Before deciding on the location where you are going
to operate your ionizer, please read the operating
instructions thoroughly and the information written
below.

The negative ions and the electrostatic field that
are being generated by your ionizers are trapping
minute pollutant particles and refresh the air. This
causes naturally dust precipitation around the
ionizer. Dust, soot and smoke particles that will
settle on the surroundings of the ionizer, are
pollutant particles and could be hazardous to your
health, while being air-borne.

The air ionizer is accelerating the percipitation
of solid pollutants from the air.

These solid pollutants that are percipitated from
the air are saved from your lungs!

Air ionizers do clean the air from pollen,
cigarette smoke, dust airborne fungal and bacterial

particles, indoor aerollergens, insecticide sprays etc. These pollutant particles and aerosols are being generated indoors and eventually will slowly settle on walls, floors, furniture etc. (and will darken them). As the natural settling takes time, the air is kept most of the time polluted, people indoors will breathe these solid pollutants!

The Air ionizer is percipitating these pollutants much faster than the natural decay. However, the dust deposit will also be noticably faster. Therefore, the surfaces on and around the air ionizer, where the ionization process is more intense, have to be cleaned frequently.

We do recommend, in our instructions, not to put the unit too near to walls (that are not washable) and to clean their surroundings frequently— so there will not be dust and soot built up.

Because of these recommended frequent cleaning of the unit and surroundings (about once a week) it is preferred to place the unit on surfaces that are washable and so will be the furniture and the walls near it. Such surfaces are: Wood, melamine, tile, glossy washable paint, washable wallpaper, wood panels, glass, polymeric material and similar surfaces. The cleaning is done by a wet cloth or a wet paper towel.

PART 2

Suggested Solutions

SUGGESTED SOLUTIONS

The following solutions to the editing exercises are, for the most part, neither the only possible solutions nor the only correct solutions. We think that they are, at least, effective solutions.

We have not suggested solutions to all the exercises because instructors in editing classes may prefer to discuss possible solutions with their students. From such discussion comes understanding—the ability to make judgments rather than apply rules.

LESSON 1. FOLLOWING CONVENTIONS

1. USING *THE CHICAGO MANUAL OF STYLE,* 14TH ED.

These are the sections containing the information.

19.11	The simplest form of strike-on composition.
4.24	The three doctrines of copyright notices.
14.17	When it is OK to use U.S.P.S. two-letter abbreviations for the names of U.S. states.
1.1	Definition of *recto* page.
11.34	Credit lines for illustrations.
7.42–7.45.i	Capitalization of topological terms
5.115	Principal use of the en dash.
10.7	Permissible changes in the handling of direct quotations.
2.186	Recommendations of useful references for editors.
Glossary	Definition of the term *epublication.*
8.67	Punctuating long numerals in scientific copy.
2.120ff	How to query authors on a manuscript.
9.133	Accents in classical Greek.
11.46	Editing captions for a list of illustrations.
2.97	Using a style sheet, with example.
18.17	The ideal line length for text meant for continuous reading.
1.47	The difference between a *foreword* and a *preface.*
12.20	Placement of table numbers.
3.19ff	Proofreaders' marks.
6.38	Hyphenating compound words.
Preface	History and purpose of the *Manual of Style.*
17.106	Alphabetizing, for an index, family names that contain particles.
13.34	Breaking displayed equations too long to fit on a single line.
16.54	Using acronyms to replace longer organizational names in text citations for reference list entries.
15.44	The advantages of endnotes over footnotes.

2. USING STANDARD EDITING MARKS

Use standard editing marks to make the unedited passage look like the edited.

Unedited Version

~~An~~ example of bit~~-~~stream customization given by ~~in~~

Le Galls ~~involved providing random access to, and the~~

~~ability to~~ edit *ing* video stored on a ~~computer~~ hard disk.

~~It was explained that one~~ requirement*s* ~~of such~~

~~operations is many~~ *random* access~~ points.~~ ~~There is the~~

~~necessity that~~ *Also,* groups of pictures *must* be coded ~~such~~ that *So* *they contain* a

fixed number of bits ~~are present to make editing~~ *How these conditions can be met*

~~possible.~~ *is*

¶ The bit stream is customized ~~which defines the~~

by The MPEG syntax ~~is achieved by having six layers in~~

~~a relationship to each other that~~ supports functions

such as DCT, motion compensation, *and* resynchronization,

and *provides the desired* random access ~~point.~~ ~~The bit stream, which is~~

~~characterized by two fields,~~ bit rate and *the* buffer size

~~is also defined by the syntax.~~ The minimum buffer size

~~necessary to decode the bit stream within the context~~
(insert on next page)

~~of~~ the video buffer verifier | is specified by | ~~the buffer size.~~ ~~It is~~ an abstract model **which** ~~of decoding used to~~ verif**ies** that an MPEG bit ∧ stream can be decoded withou**t**

u∧reasonable buffering and delay requirements. The syntax, interrelating six layers of data ∧ (insert from previous page here.)

3. ABBREVIATIONS AND MECHANICS

Edit these sentences. Watch out for multiple errors.

1. The desk was 5 ft 6 in. long. OR The desk was 5'6" long. OR The desk was five feet, six inches long.

   (The idea is to designate units and numbers consistently, following a style guide.)

2. The abbreviation for decibel is **dB**.

3. It's handy to remember that 1 in. equals 2. 54 cm.

4. You get less whisky in a 750 **ml** bottle than in a fifth.

   (You get less **whisky** [Scotch]—and for that matter, less **whiskey** [rye or bourbon].)

5. The abbreviation of hertz is **Hz**; the plural is hertz.

6. We can fix the trouble in an **average** of 5 min.

   (No reason for quotation marks on *fix*, unless you're calling the term into question. *Avg* should be spelled out in text, but your handling of *min* should be consistent with your style guide.)

7. His "farm" was only 0.06 sq. **mi**.

   (Here, the quotation marks call into question whether a plot of land only **0.06 sq mi** deserves to be called a farm.)

8. Who is going to check out the USAF pilots?

9. The **vice** president for **p**ersonnel, who was 65,
    retired.

4. EDITING FOR CONSISTENCY

For this sort of work, it's helpful to make a rough style sheet. It will help you to be consistent in your conventions for units, fractions or decimals, and product names.

The hood section used was 36 **in.** wide and 6 **ft** long at the floor level. The physical space constraints required that the detector be no more than 12 **in.** from the walls of the hood. Measurement points were chosen every 12 **in.** along both sides of the hood, to ensure full overlap, and the measurement was extended one position beyond the active area of the hood at each end. **Shots were made** parallel to the floor. The detector was placed on the floor for each shot, with the active detector centered 2½ **in.** above floor level.

The shielding for this detector caused the ~~the~~ response to drop to 50% at an angle of **26½** deg. from the centerline; thus, the 12 **in.** spacing ensured full overlap at the near wall.

The hood walls are formed of **3/16 in.** stainless steel, with 2 **in.** Benelex shielding. The attenuation of samples of Benelex ~~were~~ **was** measured, and the results were used to correct the measurement data for all inventory work as well as for this test.

(Besides editing for consistency, we corrected a dangling modifer and a subject-verb mismatch and inserted paragraphing.)

5. CHECK YOUR SPELLCHECKER

1. By **forgoing** dividends in this quarter, we can gain the needed **capital** for investment.

2. On the **advice** of **counsel**, the comptroller would say nothing about the **imminent** liability suit.

3. The author asserts that the model of ethical argumentation by analogy is better than Sawyer's legalistic model, but he never **reveals** what Sawyer's model is.

4. Because this article shows how to apply some general ethical **principles** to dilemmas in technical communication, I **definitely** plan to cite it in my paper.

5. The **straightforward** manner in which the project team presented **its** case has lead us to adopt **its** approach.

6. With **your** circuit board **lying** flat on the bench, bottom side up, solder a shunt between the pins of R37.

7. Note: the SLAM option **affects** how the **system's** conventional memory is handled.

8. Remove the rotor from the **mandrel**, then inspect the rotor to **ensure** that it is free of burrs.

9. Maintenance of **ordnance** equipment is **performed** in **Hangar** B.

10. Being unable to **breathe** under the water did not appear to **faze** the tarantula.

11. The senator's **aide**, who showed a **flair** for negotiation, urged the senator to **alter** her stand and **accept** the compromise.

12. Manufacturing will occur at **discrete sites** so that if one plant is **wracked** with labor problems, other plants can continue production.

6. CORRECT GRAMMAR

1. After the scope and cost of the effort are negotiated, **the firm will assign** experienced personnel. (Dangling modifier)

2. Remember, the guest is there **not only** to be fed but also to be entertained. (Misplaced modifier)

3. When **you** print, the page-offset feature shifts the left margin to the right. (Dangling modifier)

4. It is important that the paint cover **only** the trim. (Misplaced modifier)

5. The list shows the usual price and the students' price for the software. (Wordiness)

7. EDITING FOR CORRECTNESS

The **field** of technical communication **originated** in reaction to the neglect of **two** of **Aristotle's artistic** proofs: *pathos* and *ethos*. **T**his neglect caused managers and bureaucrats, who needed to understand technical material well enough to make decisions about **dam sites** and weapons systems, to **seek** *technical writers* who could organize and explain **technical** matters. Sometimes these **writers** were technical **people** themselves, perhaps engineers who did some reading outside **their** own field and who had a **knack** (but not a heuristic) for writing pretty well. Others were liberal arts majors who had the **interest** and patience to understand and explain technical matters, but who also lacked a heuristic, since rhetoric had largely disappeared from college curricula around 1900.

9. VERBS AND PRONOUNS

1. The committee, despite occasional disagreements, usually **functions** as an effective policy-making body.
   (Singular verb: committee acting as a unit.)

2. Rhythm and blues **has** remained a popular musical format.
   (Singular verb: R&B is a single format.)

3. Dykstra & Malone **has** moved **its** offices to the Vader building.
   (Dykstra & Malone is the singular name of a firm.)

4. Everyone **prefers their** sandwiches prepared the same way.
   (To avoid gender bias, the idiom is shifting toward *they* as an all-purpose genderless pronoun, despite gnashing of teeth among those who "know better.")

5. When it comes to salvaging my grade in physics, all **is** lost.
   ("All is lost" is idiomatic.)

6. One of the students **who** I know **is** playing soccer **comes** from Omaha.
   (*Who* is the subject of *is* in the relative clause, not the object of *know*. W*ho* also refers to *one* and requires *is*.)

0. GOTCHAS

1. During penetration, the projectile stretches the material, which snaps back afterwards. (Beware of projectiles that snap back.)

2. This situation is compromised many times for reasons of ~~time,~~ schedule or cost.

3. ~~Although t~~The history of technical communication, like **that of** its parent discipline, can stand on its own. It need not be seen ~~in an antiquarian sense~~ merely as a way to add "color and interest" to "real" technical writing. **Moreover,** ~~there is no doubt that~~ studies of early technical communication would add to the field depth, substance, and even credibility.

4. ~~Adding m~~More memory ~~lets you~~ free**s** up your computer to do other jobs.

5. The greenhouse effect traps ~~solar~~ rays from the sun, which overheat the earth.

6. The confusion that results from thoughtlessly calling a thing by different **terms** ~~names~~ seems to grow in proportion to the number of words in the . term.

11. SOME BRACKETING EXERCISES

1. Although (in circumstances)[that require exception reports in addition to the regular periodic reports], [when the due dates fall (within five days of one another)] combining an exception report (with a periodic report) is justified. ("Although," introduces a subordinate clause, but there is no main clause, so one must be created.)

Rewrite: Although circumstances may require exception reports in addition to the regular periodic reports, the two reports can be combined whenever the due dates fall within five days of one another.

2.   [What this particular piece (of machinery) is] is a precursor (of the combine).
     (The opening clause is the subject of the sentence, so both *is*es are technically necessary.)

3.   The trouble (with that hypothesis) is is{that it fails [to account (for all the observed motions)]}.
     (One *is* has no function.)

4.   When expenditures [made (for the purpose) (of acquiring additional land area) (for future utilization) (by the institution)] are accounted for (in the capital budgeting process).
     (Sentence fragment.)

     Rewrite: When the institution acquires land for future use, the expenditures are accounted for in the capital budget.

5.   {Based (on an analysis) [(of the effluents) being discharged]} there was a need {to implement measures [to mitigate the excessive presence (of arsenic)]}.

     Rewrite: Analysis of effluent discharge showed a need to mitigate the excessive presence of arsenic.

LESSON 2. USING TRANSFORMATIONAL GRAMMAR

12. ANALYZE VERB STRINGS

1. While he **was sampling** lakes for acid rain, Carl **could have been fishing**. (Past progressive, past conditional perfect progressive)

2. Fishing **has** always **been** Carl's favorite recreation. (Present perfect)

3. By May, Johnson **will have become** eligible for the health-care plan. (Present conditional perfect)

4. Tamara **had gotten** tired of always being tired at the end of her hospital shift. (Past perfect)

5. Marshall **is being** pigheaded and stubborn about seeing a tutor. (Present progressive)

6. We **are** continually surprised at the condition of the bridges on the interstates. (Present. Looks like a passive, but *surprised* is adjectival here: no unspoken agent is doing the surprising. *Surprised by* would be passive, however)

7. With this utility, making macros <u>is</u> easy. (BEj)

8. By recording your keystrokes, this utility <u>can build</u> you a macro. (Vg)

9. The next figure <u>shows</u> a macro that converts user keystrokes into macro actions. (VT)

10. Novices <u>may find</u> macros difficult to use. (Vc)

11. Sometimes a problem <u>appears</u> after many repetitions of the same command in a loop macro. (VIa)

12. Debugging <u>is</u> the process of isolating and fixing problems in a macro. (BEn)

13. The macro's problem <u>may be</u> in a faulty keystroke sequence. (BEa)

14. With longer macros, debugging <u>becomes</u> more difficult. (VIa)

15. In very long macros, debugging <u>may seem</u> an endless process. (VLn)

16.   At the end of debug mode, the debug window <u>closes</u>. (VI)

13. DIAGRAM VERB STRINGS

                    MV: Past Perf   MV: Past Perf
                         VI   VT

3. The Garcias <u>had called up</u> and <u>[had] left</u> a message on our answering machine.

         MV: Past Cond Perf Passive

      modal   aux   aux   VT

4. Marie <u>could have been called in </u>for jury duty any time last week. (Only transitive verbs can be made passive.)

         MV: Past
         BEj

5. Why <u>were</u> our plane reservations all fouled up? (Judgment call: *were fouled up* could be passive if *fouled up* described somebody's action instead of a condition.)

4. TRANSFORM SENTENCES

1. Universality of access is **not** an important health-care reform issue. (Negative sentence)

2. **Is** universality of access an important health-care reform issue? (Yes/no question)

3. **Why is** universality of access an important health-care reform issue? (Adverbial Wh-question)

4. **What** is an important health-care reform issue? (Pronoun Wh- question)

5. The issue of universal access to health care is being discussed by Congress. (Passive)

6. ~~You will~~ **W**rite your representative. ~~You will~~ **E**xpress your ideas about health-care reform. (Imperative)

7. You will write your congressional representative **and** ~~You will~~ express your ideas about health-care reform. (Compound verb)

8. **There are** many weighty and complex issues up for consideration by Congress. (Existential there)

5. IDENTIFY CORE SENTENCES

1. Atheists are in foxholes.

2. You will take two aspirin. You will call me in the morning.

3. The question on everyone's mind is [something].

4. Congress **is** capable of passing a meaningful campaign-reform bill.

5. Impoverished students **are** supposed to cope with
    higher tuition bills [in some fashion].

6. An inexperienced travel agent fouled up our plane
    reservations.

16. DIAGRAM SENTENCES TO DISCOVER STRUCTURE

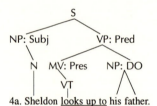

2. The President appeared at the dais.

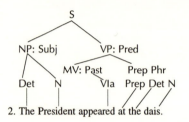

4a. Sheldon looks up to his father.

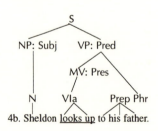

4b. Sheldon looks up to his father.

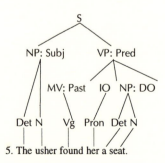

5. The usher found her a seat.

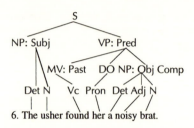

6. The usher found her a noisy brat.

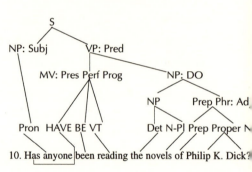

10. Has anyone been reading the novels of Philip K. Dick?

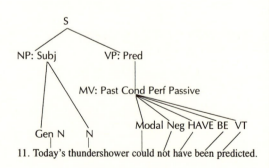

11. Today's thundershower could not have been predicted.

LESSON 3. IMPROVING SENTENCES

7. THE THEME-RHEME CONCEPT

3. In order to lay out a manual, writers should ask if the new learning is job-related or pleasure-related.

5. In California, one of the biggest concerns in any type of civil engineering is seismic activity.

7. People with AIDS were encouraged to remain working as long as the disease allowed, while co-workers were educated that the virus could not be transmitted casually.

9. At intoxicating dosages, visual problems also occur.

11. For more information on how to set the ribbon life, refer to the user manual.

13. Most fundamentally, what it means to say that one has rights is that one must not be treated as if one were a mere resource or instrument.

8. FRAMEWORK

3. As soon as users log onto the system for the first time, they will want to change their passwords.

5. If bleeding occurs, resume pressure and hold for 5 minutes.

6. If you have any questions or want more information about interacting with other technical

communicators, contact George Jones (evenings and weekends) at 555-4630.

8. Before loading the paper, verify that all the procedures in the previous chapter have been completed.

10. Once in contact with an ozone molecule, the nitrogen dioxide robs the weaker, more unstable ozone of an oxygen atom, ~~destroying the ozone molecule, which then becomes~~ **making it** a normal oxygen molecule, O_2.

19. SMOTHERED VERBS

3. Write the summary of your phase of the program so that it can be easily interpreted and compared to those of other phases.

5. Since many functions of the PC and the Macintosh are similar, we expect to be able to convert from one to the other without confusing the staff.

7. The major impacts on how the plant operates are summarized below.

9. Even though applications may improve, inherent weaknesses may accumulate to the point that the system becomes less reliable.

11. Section 4 describes how to calibrate the system.

20. MOVE THE VERB

1. Division G-7 is developing a packaging concept
    based on the use of surface-mounted electronic
    components and a high-density multilayer substrate.

3. We demonstrated the value of a light carrier with a
    multimission air wing aboard as a supplement to the
    carrier task force.

5. Also included in the course are removal and
    installation of components, testing, adjustment,
    inspection, and servicing.

7. As each up aircraft flew and returned, an "up" or
    "down" status was computed on the basis of mean
    times between maintenance actions.

21. VERBS AND EDITING

1. ~~Voice communication needs may indicate the~~
    ~~incorporation of~~ **We may need** a telephone or
    intercom.

3. Our objective is to ~~be timely in~~ meet~~ing~~ schedules
    for **supplying** information ~~and data supplied to~~
    ~~others~~.

5. The computer **software** convert**s** data from graphics
    models to the format required.

7. The principal conditions that can preclude the use
    of chem milling as a finishing operation are uneven
    thicknesses, edge rounding, and lack of flatness on
    the large planar surfaces.

22. SEPARATE VERBS FOR CLARITY

3. The chapter newsletter is one of the primary means
    of communicating news and events about the society
    and developing interest in it at the local and
    international levels.

5. You should first know the location of the major
    faults and understand their earthquake potential.

23. STACKED MODIFIERS

Stacked modifiers are underlined. If a modifier is ambiguous, it's a good idea to check
unstacked versions with the author.

3. One cannot help but wonder about the <u>software
    manufacturer's hardware system configuration
    philosophy.</u>

    **One wonders what hardware philosophy governed the
    manufacturers when they configured this software.**

5. <u>Partial-wave left-right asymmetry measurement</u> was
    accomplished by means of a <u>polarized proton target
    experimental setup.</u>

    **Left-right assymetry of partial waves was measured
    with an experimental setup using a polarized target
    for the proton bombardment.**

7. A protocol is a <u>computer to computer information
    transfer network language.</u>

    **A protocol is a language used to transfer
    information from computer to computer over a
    network.**

24. RIGHT-BRANCHING

1. During this period, the physically active child will have his share of spills, bumps, and bruises.

3. In general, the conditions are stressful—lack of exercise, isolation from other animals, lengthy confinement in tiny cages.

5. Some of the panic concerning transmission of AIDS may be diminished by offering education through public service announcements, industry bulletins, and workplace discussion groups.

7. More advisable than having a complete gun control law passed may be more narrowly targeted gun control measures, like gunowner licensing and permit-to-purchase systems.

9. In the chrono mode, the screen displays stopwatch time, showing hours, minutes, and seconds, beginning at 00.00.00.

25. PARALLELISM

1. The paper is well organized and clear and represents an important area in current policy.

3. Start up, run, and shut down the 3456 tester:

   a. Load and unload in-circuit test programs.

   b. **Run the** operational verification program.

   c. Identify fixture for items under test.

   d. Protect the device from electrostatic ~~device protection~~ **charges**.

5. Beginners in private accounting can start as ledger or cost clerks, timekeepers, or junior internal auditors, while training for technical and executive positions.

26. CREATE MORE PUNCH IN THESE SENTENCES

1. In his book, *Drinking Driving*, he discusses the deaths related to drunk driving.

3. In many people, the mere mention of AIDS causes panic.

5. In many cases, out of fear and depression, the homeless adopt bizarre behavior patterns.

7. In New York City, **among** drivers who are fatally injured, 75% have been drinking and 46% have an alcohol concentration in their blood of 0.25 or higher.

10. In a 1976 survey in India, a number of faculty and students at several colleges and universities were questioned about their preferences among the different types of English.

12. Separate steps are used, in separate locations, for laboratory sampling, inspecting, and preparing plant microfossils.

14. Other possible additions to the shuttle are structural extensions, including a service track assembly and provisions for two more crew members.

27. MARATHON SENTENCES

1. Words are powerful symbols of feeling and attitude and, as such, solid parts of the social structure.

For this reason, reformers are sometimes tempted to change the language to remedy social inequalities. But because language has the force of history behind it, any attempts to change society by censoring the language are unlikely to succeed.

3. De Broglie created the revolutionary idea that the motion of atomic particles is guided by pilot waves. However, he was too slow to develop a strict mathematical theory of this phenomenon. In 1926, about a year after de Broglie's publication, a German physicist, Erwin Schroedinger, published a general equation for de Broglie waves and proved its validity for all kinds of electron motion.

28. SENTENCE COMBINING

1. There is a greater danger from tidal waves in shallow waters than in deep waters, because the wave crest gets higher as it gets closer to shore.

3. The unit is equipped with a holster that holds the unit when it's not being used, protecting it from the damage that might occur if it were sitting loose inside the cab and also protecting the passengers from being struck by the unit in the event of an accident.

4. DMG is trying to provide an accurate earthquake scenario in inner and coastal regions to give earthquake planners an idea of the potential damage.
    (Earthquake planners, of course, don't plan earthquakes. They develop contingency plans to be used in case of earthquake.)

29. REPETITION

1. ~~Each~~ Applicants should be sure that ~~his or her~~ **their** names appear on all pages of ~~his or her~~ **their** application papers.

3. If toner is spilled, use a vacuum to clean **it** up. ~~the loose toner.~~

5. You can place the classification inside the illustration **or place it** above or below—on either side or in the center. ~~place it within the table or illustration, or place it to either side above or below the table or illustration.~~

6. ~~Although in circumstances that require exception reports in addition to the regular periodic reports, w~~When the due dates fall within five days of one another, ~~combining~~ an exception report **can be combined** with a periodic report. ~~is justified.~~

7. ~~Through the use of~~ **By using** synthetic nitrogenous fertilizers, which emit nitrogen oxides ~~into the atmosphere in the process of~~ ~~decomposing~~ into the soil **as they decompose**, farmers throughout the world added to the amount of nitrogen oxide in the air.

8. Another reason for the language differences in **colonies** ~~colonized and colonies situations~~ is the desire to maintain distance between ruler and ruled.

10. Our problem here on earth, **directly related to automobiles,** factories, ~~burning of forests and~~ coal burning, and ~~several other small factors that add up to produce a significant amount of carbon~~

~~dioxide.~~ **the burning of forests, is the abnormal
buildup of carbon dioxide in our atmosphere.**

12. ~~Extensive use of~~ Value Engineering and Life Cycle
Cost techniques will be utilized **extensively**.

14. Off-line: Not currently ~~connected to or~~ under the
control of the computer. Used to refer to equipment
such as printers and ~~disk drives,~~ information
storage media such as disks, and the information
they contain. Compare on-line.

On-line: Currently ~~connected to and~~ under the
control of the computer. ~~Used to refer to equipment
such as printers and disk drives, information
storage media such as disks, and the information
they contain.~~ Compare off-line.

15. If a clock loses, say, one second per decade, its
error may not be apparent at the end of a year. ~~or
the end of ten.~~

17. ~~Plain paper has a print side.~~ For the best ~~print~~
quality, print only on the print side of the ~~plain~~
paper. ~~The print side is not visible to the naked
eye, so before you remove the paper from a ream to
use in your printer, check the label on the end of
the ream.~~ The print side will be indicated ~~by an
arrow or other symbol~~ on the label **at the end of
the ream.** ~~Remove, undisturbed from the ream,~~ **Load**
the number of sheets ~~of paper~~ you wish to use ~~in
your printer,~~ into the media tray, print-side-down.

18. Last on the list of major **ozone-depleting**
~~depletion-causing~~ factors created by ~~man~~ **humans** is
anything containing tropospherically stable
halocarbons that contain chlorine or bromine.~~, both
of which cause depletion of the ozone.~~

20. Corrections for field procedures are always appropriate, but the overburden correction may ~~or may~~ not be ~~appropriate~~, depending on ~~the procedures used by those who developed~~ the analysis method. ~~under consideration.~~

22. On-schedule production ~~and delivery~~ of concise, accurate, **high-quality** documentation which meets all requirements is vital ~~in assuring that of the~~ **to ensure** mission performance. ~~will not be impeded by lack of the necessary technical information properly documented, or by incomplete, inaccurate, or late reports and manuals.~~

30. DOUBLETS

1. The broad range of ~~techniques and~~ processes that sometimes complicate the preparation of ~~well-designed and~~ effective presentation material can be more efficiently utilized by **professional** personnel who ~~are professionally engaged in the art and~~ have the necessary equipment. ~~and materials to do a quality job.~~

3. Codependence is any ~~suffering and/or~~ dysfunction ~~that is~~ associated with ~~results from~~ focusing on the needs ~~and behavior~~ of others.

5. The increased ~~manufacture and~~ use of computers in recent years has added many words to the English language, as well as abbreviating and eliminating ~~many~~ others.

6. Factors may include ~~mild to moderate~~ physical abuse, ~~covert or~~ less obvious mental abuse, ~~mental and~~ emotional abuse, ~~child~~ neglect, and ~~ignoring or~~

thwarting of the child's ~~spirituality or~~ spiritual growth.

8. The characteristic pits of woody elements are often preserved. ~~and also~~ **These** signify vascular plants derived from a ~~terrestrial, or~~ land-based environment.

10. A greater willingness is needed on the part of society ~~in general~~ to provide ~~adequate and~~ appropriate ~~care and~~ treatment to ~~all those who fall into the wide spectrum of~~ the mentally ill.

12. Pregnant health workers should ~~be especially familiar with and~~ strictly adhere to the universal precautions.

13. This is a dynamic documentation effort: as each new phase ~~or area~~ of the program is ~~tested and~~ completed ~~or modified~~, the appropriate documentation is ~~updated or newly~~ produced.

15. ~~Time constraints and~~ **D**ocument production schedules ~~when first imposed~~ may have ~~been~~ **seemed** reasonable **at first**, but we are confronting ~~with~~ increased task scope, better understanding of the details ~~involved as the effort progresses~~, and ~~unforeseen~~ technical problems requiring more ~~depth of~~ documentation, perhaps necessitating accelerated effort. ~~to meet schedules or to avoid delaying follow-on tasks~~.

31. CUT UNNECESSARY WORDS

1. Accounting is one of the largest fields of professional employment, with almost a half-million people. ~~working in this occupation.~~

3. Tests showed their circumferential tensile strength
   to be ~~approximately~~ 40,000 psi, well above the
   level required for long range missile**s**.
   ~~applications.~~

5. This program ~~benefits people in that it~~ will
   improve technical writing skills in ~~the areas of~~
   resumes, proposals, manuals, and **other**
   communication**s**. ~~with others.~~

7. References should be included ~~in the paper~~
   ~~sufficient~~ to enable the reader to acquire
   additional information. ~~should she desire.~~

9. It is ~~impractical and moreover~~ impossible to design
   a structure that will survive all ~~possible~~ worst-
   case scenarios.

11. Once you set the switches, you will not need to
    reset them unless you change your system ~~so that it~~
    ~~requires a different~~ configuration.

13. The ~~total amount of the~~ loan was ~~six~~ **$6** million
    ~~dollars~~.

15. These statistics ~~serve to~~ show the effects of
    inadequate supervision.

17. ~~There are~~ **S**ome products ~~that~~ have more eye appeal
    than others.

19. Familiarity with ~~the methods whereby~~ printing
    operations ~~can be performed~~ is highly beneficial.

21. ~~The field of~~ **In** economics, ~~is one in which~~ computer
    studies have often been ~~used~~ successful~~ly~~.

23. ~~To obtain the best possible results in the~~
    ~~application of~~ **In** desktop publishing it is
    sometimes **necessary** to modify the procedures ~~for~~

~~using the software in order~~ to suit ~~the
characteristics and practical requirements of~~
particular users.

25. The effects of gaseous composition on ~~the
determination of~~ convective heating rates is **well**
known ~~to a comparatively high degree~~.

27. ~~Consideration will be given to a~~Advertising
effectiveness **will be considered in relation** to ~~a
degree consistent with the definition of~~ costs
~~expended~~.

29. A test plan will be defined for obtaining the
medical data ~~which is not presently available but
which is~~ necessary in order to utilize ~~the each of~~
the pharmaceuticals on **the** elderly ~~populations~~.

31. The ~~planned~~ approach for defini**ng** ~~tion of~~ the new
~~and/or modified~~ operating requirements ~~identified
above~~ is ~~essentially~~ outlined above.

33. To enter the competition, submit a**n** ~~completed~~ entry
form.

35. Figure 6-1 ~~provides an illustration of~~ **shows** the
cable.

37. Adults become ready to learn when they experience
~~in their life situation a need to know or~~ a need ~~to
be able to do something in order~~ to perform more
effectively ~~and satisfyingly~~.

38. The ~~fact of the matter is that the~~ office does not
have enough time ~~in its~~ allot**ted** ~~ment to make
expenditures on~~ **for such** programs ~~of this nature~~.

40. Those maintaining that such tight bureaucratic
    regulation is necessary to stabilize both prices
    and production should be the most diligent in
    support ~~of the development and utilization of all~~
    ~~forms or organizations and of procedures available~~
    ~~for peaceful resolution of the conflict between the~~
    ~~various segments~~ of ~~the industry, such as~~
    arbitration ~~and conciliation~~.

32. ADD WORDS

1. Document the procedures, note complications, and
   record distal pulses, along with the patient's age

2. Since 80% of jobs are found indirectly, begin
   networking **early,** before you begin seeking a
   position.

3. We propose 1) a surface-floating bridge or 2) an
   underwater bridge suspended from **pylons mounted on**
   the ocean bottom.

33. SEQUENCE

1. A 30 in. by 30 in. cutaway may be very effective in
   a repair manual, but if in its published form it is
   reduced to a 2 in. by 2 in. square, it does not
   communicate.

3. Technical writers are there to help new and
   seasoned consultants alike to practice their trade
   more effectively.

5. Joseph Brown will give a presentation on technology
   transfer.

4. USELESS CATEGORIES

3. This particular piece of machinery is a precursor
    of the combine.

5. Although most zinc-bearing ores in the Upper Congo
    occur in conjunction with the ores of other metals,
    in the Ntagwe district they do not.

6. The following graphic software is highly
    recommended for technical reports.

8. Judges evaluate newsletters by considering the
    following: size and frequency; choice of topics,
    such as meeting notices and reports, feature
    articles, and chapter activities; editorial
    quality, including usage and style; and title and
    page design.

5. METADISCOURSE

1. It is common for the sky to become cloudy when it
    rains.

2. Before discussing the actual problems that may
    occur, this chapter examines the PC's memory system
    in great detail. Until the PC is properly
    reconfigured, most changes in memory capacity will
    create an apparent system error during POST.

6. THE EDITOR AS A HEDGE TRIMMER

1. ~~It is important to note that~~ **In** the application of
    the theory to particular situations, it may be
    necessary ~~in many cases~~ ~~to make adjustments~~ to
    compensate for exogenous factors.

2. ~~To listen~~ **Listening** to ~~and analyze successive groups of~~ supervisors' ~~diagnose, discuss, and~~ attempt**s** to resolve their communication problems inevitably leads ~~to the consideration of~~ **us to consider** whether ~~many or most of what we call~~ **such** problems ~~(and perceive as such)~~ might not be symptoms of other difficulties. ~~which exist betwee~~ ~~persons and groups.~~

37. FAULTY STRUCTURE

1. The valve configuration that was finally decided upon was a pneumatically operated ball-type valve, controlled by a solenoid.

3. Ozone is most concentrated at about 25 kilometers, but it can be detected as high as 50 kilometers.

5. Before moving the system to its operating location check overhead, side, and corner turn clearances along the planned route and confirm that all necessary facilities are available for unobstructe passage.

7. With the growth of urban areas, the Industrial Revolution began an era of unprecedented economic advances, but at the cost of harming one major resource, the earth.

9. In 1993, a study reported that 7.8% of 858 women visiting a university's student health care facility for routine gynecological examination had previously experienced unwanted sexual activity.

11. Technical writing not only is an integral part of engineering communication but it also affects the entire profession.

'8. DECIDE WHAT ELSE IS NOT NEEDED

2. In communications theory, superfluous information
    is called "noise." It is semantic noise, similar to
    engineering noise such as static from equipment.

3. The impact of negative slides on visibility and
    viewer attention is clearly favorable.

5. Those who are new to computer graphics may feel
    overwhelmed by the amount of information available.
    To help relieve their anxiety, start by introducing
    the capabilities and costs.

9. INFERRING MEANING FROM SYNTACTIC CLUES

1. Whenever a zygoplam trigloptrerizes a set of
    demonuperted tragloglumps, clausteriggled
    permagloze will maklerate multifrangible
    monopigsimules.

Sentences 2-4 are plausible variations on the first sentence, such as might be used in different paragraph contexts. Sentences 5–8 have some combination of the problems you've been working on in the exercises on smothered verbs, sequence, etc.

Sentence 11 is inconsistent, and 13 is questionable. Sentence 11 has the ognivator as the cause of glirpening, whereas sentences 9 and 10 suggest fribbled frammises as the cause. One method of checking relationships is to substitute known words for unknown ones, e.g., "When the gasoline of a car becomes rotten, the orifice of the metering jet is likely to clog." For sentence 11, you'd get "A car whose gas is rotten may clog the metering jet's orifice," obviously wrong. Sentence 13 is questionable because it obscures the relation of riplogle to zyfling birklet.

0. EDITING POMPOSITY

2. We plan to ask customers how they might use media.
    Then we will incorporate that information into our
    plans for training customer personnel.

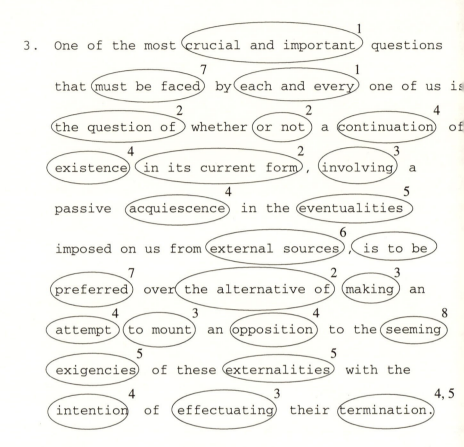

3. One of the most (crucial and important) questions
    that (must be faced) by (each and every) one of us is
    (the question of) whether (or not) a (continuation) of
    (existence) (in its current form), (involving) a
    passive (acquiescence) in the (eventualities)
    imposed on us from (external sources), (is to be)
    (preferred) over (the alternative of) (making) an
    (attempt) (to mount) an (opposition) to the (seeming)
    (exigencies) of these (externalities) with the
    (intention) of (effectuating) their (termination.)

1 - Doublets	5 - Pompous, vague nouns
2 - Redundancies	6 - Wordiness
3 - Flabby verbs	7 - Unnecessary passive voice
4 - Smothered verbs	8 - Hedges

Following the suggestions made so far, you might reduce the pompous passage to something like this:

> One of the most important questions each of us
> faces is whether to continue passively acquiescing
> to external events, or to oppose external forces,
> intending to end them.

Of course, William Shakespeare expressed the idea more memorably in *Hamlet*:

> To be, or not to be: that is the question.

> Whether 'tis nobler in the mind to suffer

The slings and arrows of outrageous fortune,

Or to take arms against a sea of troubles,

And by opposing end them. (III, i)

f we can't do it as well as Shakespeare, we can at least be less wordy than the
ureaucratese "translation."

41. THE IRISH BULL

(Warning: these sentences have lost some perverse charm in the editing.)

1. I came around to see you, and you were gone.

3. In one year there were 580,000 cases where handguns
    were used, including minor assaults in which the
    gun was not fired.

5. Start/stop timer button: This button performs the
    named functions.

7. Information on changing the battery will not be
    mentioned here, so please note the caution and
    recommendations in the battery-replacement section.

9. A small part of the depletion the ozone suffers can
    be attributed to the space shuttle. This is ironic,
    since the shuttle has done a vast amount of
    atmospheric research.

11. His writing skills are not the greatest, and any
    sort of help in this area is worth the effort.

13. I have little knowledge in technical writing, but I
    do have experience in creative and expository
    writing.

42. ZEUGMA (FALSE PARALLELISM)

Humorless versions:

1.   He took his hat and coat, and he left.

3.   "Probably there had never been such a mingling of
     art, sex, politics, spiritualism, cold meats, and
     lettuce sandwiches."

     (Zeugma used intentionally: let it stand.)

5.   For critiques, images can be enhanced, moved, and
     enlarged with computer graphics.

8.   Typically, the only way one finds out about the
     unadvertised costs and hears the horror stories is
     by word of mouth.

LESSON 4. IMPROVING PARAGRAPHS

43. REORGANIZE PARAGRAPHS USING THE INCHWORM CONCEPT

1. In the earth's crust, the second most abundant element is silicon. Silicon is the primary ingredient in sand.

3. The struggle to define the unique qualities of technical writing began considerably earlier. During the scientific revolution of the seventeenth century, Royal Society members promoted a "plain" style. Flowery language and convoluted sentence structure were deemed inappropriate.

5. A frog's heart can be kept alive and beating outside its body by immersing it in Ringer's solution. (The solution is named after the English physician Sidney Ringer, who made this discovery in 1882.) The solution contains, in about the proportions found in frogs' blood, some trace minerals in addition to sodium, potassium, and calcium. Each mineral is somehow essential for muscle function.

44. KEEP THE TOPIC FORWARD

3. Eighteen former plutonium workers were the subjects of a special study. Their lymphocyte-subtype classifications were reviewed in relation to their radiation sensitivity. For these subjects, elevated T-cell helper/suppressor ratios were higher than for the 14 age-matched controls.

4. All the attention given in the press to object-oriented languages sometimes obscures the fact that as computing environments change, older program languages continue to change. In particular, Fortran is going through a growth spurt. This growth in Fortran-based applications has fueled demand for a better Fortran. And a new Fortran standard, Fortran 90, has just been brought forth by a joint ANSI-ISO committee.

45. READER IMPACT, UNITY, COHERENCE

Although Acme could stop financing the dealers, it should continue to finance them.

Cutting off the dealers would reduce expenditures by about $1 million per year, perhaps reducing capital commitments. Without this expense, the sales necessary to produce a 15 percent return are calculated to be down 16 percent (Table 1).

However, not offering financing would make dealers hard to come by. It would also, in all probability, reduce sales from the levels shown in Table 1, because dealers would not have enough equipment to produce a variety of structures.

46. MULTIPLE PROBLEMS

1. As noted earlier, retinal mobility is one factor eye surgeons consider before employing the operation of Custodis and Lincoff. This procedure makes it possible to reattach retinas without draining the retinal fluid.

Surgeons assess the mobility of the detached
retina on the basis of two factors: the depth of
the subretinal fluid and the longitudinal extent of
the retinal separation. If the depth of fluid is
<10 mm and the length of retinal separation exceeds
1.5 mm, they will probably decide that Custodis-
Lincoff is contraindicated.

2. Why do social systems evolve at all? Why do they
   evolve from tribe to chiefdom to state? Most
   particularly, why do individual households abide by
   an implicit social contract in which their surplus
   time is appropriated by other households?

   This evolution, according to one author, occurs
   because of rising population densities. Social
   integration, he argues, is closely related to the
   technology of communication and transportation. For
   each technological level of communication or
   transportation, the size of the territory
   integrated imposes a practical limit to effective
   social integration. Hence, the only way more people
   can be incorporated into a social system is by
   increasing the number of people per square mile.

   This theory, however, fails to explain why, as
   population density increases, we do not simply have
   social fission—that is, more societies of the same
   size, rather than larger social systems. This is
   the crucial issue this paper addresses.

3. MERIT PROMOTION PROGRAM

   A major improvement has been made in selecting
   candidates for merit promotions. The underwriting
   and supervisory judgment tests have been replaced

by a new supervisory evaluation system. The new Job
Factor Profile eliminates total numerical scores
and permits a precise evaluation through a scale of
nine degrees of merit, covering different kinds of
positions.

4. LIGHTING FIXTURE LAMPS

A form No. 94-5932 was submitted to your office on
June 18 for lighting fixture lamps for the Wichita
office building. However, we requested that
procurement was to await the awarding of a contract.
Now that the Coleman Company has been awarded the
contract, the lamps can be procured.

However, other lamps are now also required. The
following list consolidates our requirements.

The cost of all the lamps is chargeable to the
accounting symbols appearing on the X-200,
authorization for $50,000, dated September 1, that
was given to Mrs. Apple on September 30.

47. DETAIL

2. A pair of electromagnetic coils is mounted behind
    each hammer and wound around each pole piece. When
    hammer drive logic determines that the hammer must
    print a dot, a current pulse energizes the coils.
    The hammer springs forward, strikes the ribbon and
    leaves a dot impression on the paper.

3. To a chemist, fire is a form of oxidation in which
    excess oxygen combines with other elements.

4. If you filed your quarterly tax, there should be a
    record of it in the regional IRS office.

48. PRECISION

1. Forests have a large percentage of living biomass, but tree trunks in a forest don't exchange carbon as much as leaves do. Therefore, the ratio of biomass to productivity is much larger than in a savannah.

3. Carbon dioxide is a main factor in the function of the greenhouse effect, the process which helps trap the radiation from the sun and raises temperatures harmfully.

5. Because of inadequate instruments for calculating amounts of ozone, scientists were at first unable to identify the hole over Antarctica.

LESSON 5. IMPROVING LONGER DOCUMENTS

49. EDIT SUMMARY

Many of the persons interviewed indicated a need for
training that would better equip supervisors to counsel
and motivate workers and, where appropriate, to
discipline workers constructively. Additional details
relating to this need appear in the section "Employee
and Supervisory Effectiveness."

A number of the interviewees complained of
occasional discrimination in tryouts for the on-the-job
training that improves opportunities for advancement.

50. EDIT SHORT REPORT

TRAINING SURVEY (Management version)

The annual training survey has some weaknesses that
should be eliminated.

Presently, the Personnel and Training Division is
given only the total numerical needs for courses. No
names are submitted, although area, branch, and
regional divisional training coordinators all have this
information. There is no indication that the training
is related to the reported need on employee appraisal
forms, or that training priorities have been
established with the region or with specific
organizations.

By the year 2000, an automated system will be
available which will show the kind of training each
individual has had and the courses needed. The new

system will improve the annual needs survey and update the individual training records. However, the region will still have to establish priorities both for courses and for the employees selected to take them.

TRAINING SURVEY (Announcement to employees)

A new, automated system will soon be in place to keep track of the training you have already had. The system will help management in the region decide who needs what training.

The new system will solve a couple of problems. It will link the training needs reported on employee appraisal forms to the numerical needs reported to the Personnel and Training Division by the training coordinators in area branches and divisions. It will also consolidate these reported needs for existing courses with requests and proposals for new ones.

51. EDIT SHORT ARTICLE

COMPUTERS IN DESIGN AND PRINTING

Recent advances have opened up a new world of art, design, and other visual applications for computers. Computer graphics have been expanded for use in engineering and drafting, and for making charts for reports and slides for speakers.

The advantages of using computers in design are readily apparent. Computers solve problems in less time and provide visible alternatives. They can reduce turnaround time and cut costs. For example, on a satellite run of a U.S. military program, a problem occurred in analyzing returning satellite data. Without computer graphics it took one month to calculate results. With computer graphics it took 48 hours.

The benefits of using computer graphics include productivity, creativity, and speed.

Images can be enhanced, moved, or enlarged, relieving users of repetitive design tasks while increasing their productivity. Costly mistakes can be reduced, since design alternatives can be reviewed for selection in advance. Trial-and-error solutions can be reviewed in a fraction of the time that would be needed for conventional means.

One of the industries using computer graphics is printing. In print shops and on newspapers and magazines, the typesetter uses a computer to set the type (phototypesetting), replacing the old hot lead type method.

Computers are also being used to control presses, making it possible to adjust colors on massive runs, particularly on newspapers. They can refine and manipulate images, and even create finished artwork from initial roughs. They can also automate manual operations, increasing productivity.

The fastest area of growth for printing firms is in color separation. One of the firms doing this extensively by computer is Microtype, Inc. Although the cost of separating a single job can run as high as $1000, when compared with the same job done manually it is produced in one-tenth the time and with greater accuracy.

Unfortunately, the most sophisticated computer programs are now prohibitively expensive. But as the technology expands, the reduced cost of computer memory, processing, and available mass-produced technology will likely reduce prices overall.

52. WHAT DO READERS REALLY NEED TO KNOW?

Since this manual is packed inside a box along with the product, there's not much need for hype. Since the pump is fully assembled and is too cheap to be worth stocking parts for, there's no need to describe the assembly. Most people who buy it will already understand how to use it, so there's no need to provide elaborate operating instructions.

It wouldn't hurt to include diagrams—operation and details of the thumb chuck with tire valve and sporting-goods needle.

Readers should certainly be alerted about the pump's intended uses and its rated capacity, if only to prevent product-liability problems.

Hand-Operated Airpump

Congratulations on your purchase of this high-quality airpump. With proper use, it will give you many years of service.

Uses: inflating bicycle tires and sporting goods such as basketballs, footballs, and lightweight rubber rafts.

Maximum capacity: 60 psi (pounds per square inch).

To inflate tires:

- Clamp the hose nozzle onto the filler stem of the tire to be inflated.

- Stand on the toe plate.

- Pump the plunger up and down to inflate the tire with air.

To inflate sporting goods:

* Insert the big end of the supplied filler needle into the nozzle clamp.

* Moisten the needle and insert it into the ball's navel.

* Stand on the toe plate.

* Pump the plunger up and down to inflate the ball with air.

53. EDIT JOB DESCRIPTION

JOB DESCRIPTION

I am responsible for expediting the assembly of the Aircraft Fuel System and associated tankage, tubes, and fittings. I have to determine the status of hardware (by part number) and ensure that it meets its delivery date on each aircraft (by serial number).

I make weekly status reports, reviewing the progress of vendor and in-house assembly against the need dates furnished by the planning department. I also review the following:

Buyers' and Engineers' ACIEs

Purchase order changes

Hardware test failures

MRRs

Failure analysis

Lab and qualification test reports

Manufacturing schedule progress reports

Production and spares support shortage lists

Procurement requests

ECPs

Air Force changes

Volatile systems, such as this one, require many repairs, retrofits, and design changes. I therefore maintain close contact with engineering procurement, reliability, and production control, reviewing many of their reports to get information.

On outstanding shortages, I contact vendors daily for their shipping dates. To overcome shortages, I sometimes shift hardware, adjusting assembly dates and expediting where possible. When shortages affect the master schedule, I seek corrective action with the systems manager or Production Control.

As part of my job, I also draw up charts and graphs for management and the Air Force, take field trips, make recommendations and proposals, and write reports and memos.

54. EDIT USER MANUAL

This exercise tests your diplomatic skills as well as your editing skills. In that letter to the client, you might wish to take a less direct approach than you would with an American client. Since the ionizer's action and the client's concern for the buyer's understanding are both praiseworthy, praise them. Call your changes "suggestions," and assure the client that your goal, like his, is to make sure that buyers understand and appreciate this fine product.

In this case, you would probably not present the client with a marked-up draft. Instead, lay the page out carefully and show only the results of the editing—something on the order of the finished page for the hand-operated airpump.

WITHDRAWN

No longer the property of the
Boston Public Library.
Sale of this material benefits the Library